We hope this book has been informative and helpful on your journey to understanding and celebrating older adults. Thank you for your interest and support!

Title: The Pioneers: Unleashing the Power of PoW

Subtitle: Exploring the Trailblazers of Pure Proof-of-Work Coins

Series: Trailblazers of the Blockchain: Unleashing the Power of PoW

By Alexander C. Blair

Table of Contents

Understanding the Evolution of Cryptocurrencies

In recent years, the world has witnessed a remarkable transformation in the realm of finance and technology with the emergence of cryptocurrencies. Cryptocurrencies, also known as digital currencies, have revolutionized the way we perceive and engage in financial transactions. At the heart of this transformation lies the groundbreaking technology called blockchain, a decentralized and immutable ledger that forms the backbone of most cryptocurrencies.

In order to fully appreciate the significance of cryptocurrencies, it is essential to understand their evolutionary journey. This chapter aims to provide a comprehensive overview of the evolution of cryptocurrencies, from their humble beginnings to the global phenomenon they have become today. By exploring the key milestones, technological advancements, and influential factors that shaped their development, we can gain a deeper understanding of their impact on the financial landscape.

1. The Birth of Bitcoin

The story of cryptocurrencies begins with the introduction of Bitcoin, the first decentralized digital currency. In 2008, an enigmatic figure known as Satoshi Nakamoto published a whitepaper titled "Bitcoin: A Peer-to-

Peer Electronic Cash System." This groundbreaking document outlined the concept of a digital currency that operates without the need for intermediaries, such as banks or governments.

Bitcoin's underlying technology, known as blockchain, provided a transparent and secure method for recording transactions. Through a consensus mechanism called Proof-of-Work (PoW), Bitcoin established a decentralized network of computers that verified and validated transactions, ensuring their immutability and integrity.

2. The Rise of Altcoins

As Bitcoin gained popularity and recognition, it paved the way for the emergence of alternative cryptocurrencies, often referred to as altcoins. These altcoins sought to address certain limitations or introduce novel features not present in Bitcoin.

One of the earliest altcoins to gain traction was Litecoin (LTC), often referred to as "the silver to Bitcoin's gold." Created by Charlie Lee in 2011, Litecoin aimed to improve upon Bitcoin's transaction speed and scalability. It introduced several technical enhancements, including a different hashing algorithm and a shorter block generation time, making it a more efficient alternative.

3. Diversification and Innovation

With the success of Litecoin, the floodgates opened, leading to an explosion of new cryptocurrencies each offering unique features and use cases. Peercoin (PPC), established in 2012, pioneered the concept of a hybrid consensus mechanism called Proof-of-Stake (PoS), which aimed to address some of the environmental concerns associated with PoW by reducing energy consumption.

Around the same time, Bytecoin (BCN) introduced an enhanced focus on privacy, aiming to create an untraceable digital currency. Subsequent cryptocurrencies such as Monero (XMR) and Zcash (ZEC) further advanced the field of privacy-centric cryptocurrencies, implementing cutting-edge technologies like Ring Signatures and Zero-Knowledge Proofs.

4. Expansion and Maturation

As the cryptocurrency ecosystem expanded, various cryptocurrencies focused on specific niches and use cases. Dash emerged as a digital currency that emphasized speed and anonymity, while Vertcoin sought to maintain decentralization by resisting specialized mining hardware known as ASICs.

In addition to these advancements, the growing adoption of cryptocurrencies in the mainstream financial industry has led to increased regulatory attention and the development of stablecoins—cryptocurrencies pegged to traditional assets to reduce volatility.

5. The Future of Cryptocurrencies

As we look to the future, the evolution of cryptocurrencies shows no signs of slowing down. The technology behind cryptocurrencies, blockchain, has the potential to disrupt numerous industries beyond finance, including supply chain management, healthcare, and voting systems. Furthermore, advancements in scalability, interoperability, and privacy are expected to propel cryptocurrencies into wider adoption and mainstream acceptance.

Conclusion

Understanding the evolution of cryptocurrencies provides us with valuable insights into their transformative power and potential. From the birth of Bitcoin to the rise of altcoins and the ongoing innovation in the field, cryptocurrencies have reshaped our perception of money, finance, and trust. The journey of cryptocurrencies is a testament to human ingenuity, technological progress, and the relentless pursuit of a decentralized future.

In the following chapters, we will delve into the untold stories of specific cryptocurrencies that emerged as trailblazers during the early blockchain era. By exploring their visionary concepts, technical advancements, market adoption, and impact on the broader crypto landscape, we will gain a deeper appreciation for the pioneers who shaped the future of digital finance. Let us embark on a captivating journey through the world of Proof-of-Work coins and unleash their transformative power.

In the world of cryptocurrencies, consensus mechanisms play a vital role in maintaining the integrity and security of transactions. Among the various consensus mechanisms employed, Proof-of-Work (PoW) stands as one of the most well-known and widely used. PoW not only powers the decentralized nature of cryptocurrencies but also provides a mechanism for achieving consensus without relying on a central authority. This chapter delves into the significance of Proof-of-Work, its underlying principles, and its impact on the evolution of cryptocurrencies.

1. Understanding Consensus Mechanisms

Consensus mechanisms are the fundamental building blocks that enable distributed networks to reach an agreement on the state of a shared ledger, such as a blockchain. In traditional centralized systems, a central authority ensures consensus by validating and recording transactions. However, in decentralized systems like cryptocurrencies, consensus must be achieved in a trustless and distributed manner.

2. Introducing Proof-of-Work

Proof-of-Work was introduced by Satoshi Nakamoto as the consensus mechanism for Bitcoin, and it has since become synonymous with the security and integrity of blockchain networks. At its core, PoW is a computational puzzle that network participants, known as miners, must solve to validate transactions and add them to the blockchain.

3. How Proof-of-Work Works

To comprehend the significance of PoW, it is crucial to understand its inner workings. Miners in a PoW-based system compete to solve complex mathematical puzzles, requiring substantial computational power and energy consumption. The first miner to solve the puzzle is granted the authority to add a block of transactions to the blockchain and is rewarded with newly minted coins as an incentive.

4. Security and Immunity to Attacks

One of the primary advantages of PoW is its inherent security. By requiring miners to invest computational resources and solve puzzles, PoW ensures that an attacker would need to control a majority of the network's computing power, known as a 51% attack, to manipulate the blockchain. This robust security feature has made PoW-based cryptocurrencies resilient against various attacks, including double-spending and tampering with transaction history.

5. Energy Consumption and Environmental Impact

While PoW has demonstrated its effectiveness in securing blockchain networks, it has also attracted criticism due to its high energy consumption. The computational power required for solving PoW puzzles consumes significant amounts of electricity, leading to concerns about the environmental impact of cryptocurrencies. However, it is essential to note that efforts are being made to develop more energy-efficient consensus mechanisms and explore alternative energy sources for mining operations.

6. PoW and the Evolution of Cryptocurrencies

Proof-of-Work has played a pivotal role in the evolution of cryptocurrencies beyond Bitcoin. Numerous altcoins, including Litecoin, Ethereum, and Monero, have adopted PoW as their consensus mechanism, benefiting from its proven security and decentralization. PoW has facilitated the growth of vibrant mining communities, fostered innovation in hardware and software development, and contributed to the establishment of robust and resilient blockchain networks.

7. Criticisms and Alternative Consensus Mechanisms

While PoW remains popular, it is not without its critics. Concerns about its energy consumption, centralization tendencies, and potential for mining monopolies have led to the exploration of alternative consensus mechanisms. Proof-of-Stake (PoS), Delegated Proof-of-Stake (DPoS), and Practical Byzantine Fault

Tolerance (PBFT) are some of the alternative approaches that aim to address the limitations of PoW.

Conclusion

Proof-of-Work has played a foundational role in the development and proliferation of cryptocurrencies. Its significance lies in its ability to provide a secure, decentralized, and immutable ledger, enabling trustless transactions and fostering innovation in the blockchain space. While challenges such as energy consumption and centralization persist, PoW continues to be a prominent consensus mechanism, and its impact on the evolution of cryptocurrencies cannot be overstated. In the following chapters, we will explore the trailblazing cryptocurrencies that harnessed the power of PoW to shape the crypto landscape we know today.

In the early days of blockchain technology and cryptocurrencies, a handful of pioneering coins emerged as trailblazers, each contributing unique features and innovations to the rapidly evolving crypto landscape. These coins, built on the foundation of Proof-of-Work (PoW), not only expanded the possibilities of digital finance but also paved the way for the countless cryptocurrencies that followed.

This chapter serves as an introduction to the remarkable pioneers that will be explored in detail throughout this book. By shedding light on their origins, key features, and contributions, we aim to provide a glimpse into the transformative power of these coins and the impact they had on the broader blockchain industry.

1. Bitcoin (BTC)

No discussion of pioneering cryptocurrencies would be complete without mentioning Bitcoin, the groundbreaking digital currency that started it all. Introduced by the mysterious Satoshi Nakamoto in 2009, Bitcoin revolutionized the concept of money by creating a decentralized, peer-to-peer electronic cash system. Its key attributes, such as transparency, security, and scarcity, laid the foundation for the subsequent coins that emerged.

2. Litecoin (LTC)

Litecoin, often referred to as "the silver to Bitcoin's gold," emerged in 2011 as one of the first altcoins. Created by Charlie Lee, a former Google engineer, Litecoin aimed to address some of the limitations of Bitcoin, particularly in terms of transaction speed and scalability. With a shorter block generation time and a different hashing algorithm, Litecoin offered a faster and more efficient alternative while maintaining the core principles of decentralization.

3. Peercoin (PPC)

Introduced in 2012, Peercoin brought a new concept to the cryptocurrency world with its sustainable and energy-efficient approach. Created by Sunny King and Scott Nadal, Peercoin incorporated a hybrid consensus mechanism called Proof-of-Stake (PoS) alongside PoW. By combining the two, Peercoin aimed to reduce energy consumption and promote a more environmentally friendly approach to securing the blockchain.

4. Bytecoin (BCN)

Bytecoin, established in 2012, sought to address the crucial aspect of privacy within cryptocurrency transactions. By implementing the Cryptonote protocol, Bytecoin introduced features such as ring signatures and stealth addresses, enabling users to conduct transactions with a higher degree of anonymity and untraceability. It laid the groundwork for subsequent privacy-centric coins that prioritized user confidentiality.

5. Monero (XMR)

Building upon the foundation laid by Bytecoin, Monero emerged in 2014 as a truly private, secure, and untraceable cryptocurrency. Monero introduced innovative features such as Ring Confidential Transactions (RingCT) and Stealth Addresses, which obfuscated transaction details and shielded user identities. With a strong focus on privacy and fungibility, Monero positioned itself as a leading choice for individuals seeking enhanced confidentiality in their financial transactions.

6. Zcash (ZEC)

In 2016, Zcash entered the scene, further advancing the realm of privacy-protecting cryptocurrencies. Built on a technology called zk-SNARKs (zero-knowledge proofs), Zcash allowed users to conduct fully encrypted transactions while still maintaining the transparency of a public blockchain. This unique approach struck a balance between privacy and regulatory compliance, opening up new possibilities for confidential transactions in a regulated world.

Conclusion

The pioneers of PoW-based cryptocurrencies laid the groundwork for the transformative power of blockchain technology and digital finance. From the inception of Bitcoin to the emergence of Litecoin, Peercoin, Bytecoin, Monero, and Zcash, each coin brought forth unique features and perspectives that pushed the boundaries of what was possible in the crypto landscape.

In the upcoming chapters, we will delve deeper into the individual stories of these trailblazing coins, exploring their origins, technical advancements, market adoption, and impact on the broader blockchain industry. Join us as we uncover the triumphs, challenges, and breakthroughs that shaped the crypto landscape we know today and witness the relentless pursuit of innovation, privacy, and security that forever changed the realm of digital finance.

Chapter 1: Litecoin (LTC), established 2011 - "The silver to Bitcoin's gold."

Early Origins and the Vision of "Silver to Bitcoin's Gold"

Litecoin (LTC) emerged in 2011 as one of the earliest altcoins, introducing a unique perspective on the cryptocurrency landscape. Created by Charlie Lee, a former Google engineer, Litecoin aimed to address some of the limitations of Bitcoin while maintaining the core principles of decentralization and security. This section delves into the early origins of Litecoin and explores its vision as "the silver to Bitcoin's gold."

1. The Genesis of Litecoin

The story of Litecoin begins with Charlie Lee, who, inspired by Bitcoin's success, recognized the potential for further advancements in the world of cryptocurrencies. Lee set out to create a digital currency that could complement Bitcoin's strengths and offer additional benefits. With a background in software engineering and a deep understanding of blockchain technology, Lee embarked on a mission to develop a cryptocurrency that could serve as a viable alternative.

2. The Need for "Silver to Bitcoin's Gold"

As Bitcoin gained prominence, some inherent limitations became apparent. Bitcoin's transaction confirmation times and block generation intervals were relatively slow, limiting its scalability and efficiency. Recognizing this, Charlie Lee envisioned Litecoin as a cryptocurrency that could act as a complementary counterpart to Bitcoin, providing faster transaction confirmations and increased scalability. This vision led to Litecoin's positioning as "the silver to Bitcoin's gold."

3. Technical Features and Advancements

Litecoin introduced several technical features and advancements that set it apart from Bitcoin. One notable difference was Litecoin's adoption of the Scrypt hashing algorithm, which offered advantages over Bitcoin's SHA-256 algorithm. Scrypt allowed for faster block generation times and facilitated efficient mining on consumer-grade hardware. Additionally, Litecoin implemented a different total supply, with four times the number of coins compared to Bitcoin, leading to a higher maximum supply of 84 million LTC.

4. Market Adoption and Community Development

Litecoin's early days were marked by active community engagement and growing adoption. As a prominent altcoin, it garnered attention from early adopters and cryptocurrency enthusiasts seeking an alternative to Bitcoin. Litecoin's faster transaction confirmations and lower fees made it particularly appealing for day-to-day transactions. Over time, the Litecoin community grew, attracting developers, miners, and investors who contributed to its development and ecosystem.

5. Impact on the Cryptocurrency Ecosystem

Litecoin's entry into the cryptocurrency ecosystem had a significant impact on the industry as a whole. As one of the first altcoins, Litecoin demonstrated that there was room for innovation and differentiation beyond Bitcoin. Its technical advancements, such as faster block generation times and efficient mining, paved the way for subsequent cryptocurrencies. Moreover, Litecoin's success inspired the development of numerous other "lite" variants and alternative cryptocurrencies.

6. Collaborations and Synergies

Litecoin's journey was not just about competition with Bitcoin but also about collaboration and synergies within the crypto space. Over the years, Litecoin has formed strategic partnerships and collaborations with various blockchain projects and businesses. These collaborations have aimed to enhance interoperability, expand adoption, and drive innovation across different cryptocurrencies, contributing to the overall growth of the blockchain ecosystem.

Conclusion

The early origins of Litecoin and its vision as "the silver to Bitcoin's gold" showcased the potential for innovation and differentiation within the cryptocurrency landscape. Charlie Lee's vision of creating a faster, more scalable cryptocurrency resonated with a growing community of enthusiasts and paved the way for subsequent altcoins. Litecoin's technical features, market adoption, and impact on the cryptocurrency ecosystem solidified its position as one of the pioneering cryptocurrencies, and its journey continues to shape the ever-evolving world of digital finance.

Litecoin (LTC) emerged as a trailblazing cryptocurrency in 2011, introducing technical features and advancements that differentiated it from Bitcoin and contributed to its unique position as "the silver to Bitcoin's gold." This section explores the technical aspects that set Litecoin apart, including its hashing algorithm, block generation time, maximum supply, and other innovative developments.

1. The Scrypt Hashing Algorithm

One of the key technical differentiators of Litecoin is its adoption of the Scrypt hashing algorithm. While Bitcoin utilizes the SHA-256 algorithm, Litecoin opted for Scrypt to achieve its goals of faster block generation times and improved efficiency. Scrypt was specifically designed to be memory-intensive, making it more resistant to ASIC (Application-Specific Integrated Circuit) mining. This decision democratized mining, allowing a wider range of participants to engage in the process using consumer-grade hardware.

2. Faster Block Generation Times

Litecoin introduced faster block generation times compared to Bitcoin. While Bitcoin targets a block time of approximately 10 minutes, Litecoin's target block time is 2.5

minutes. This four-fold reduction in block time significantly improved transaction confirmations, making Litecoin more suitable for day-to-day transactions. The faster block generation times also contributed to increased network throughput and scalability, enabling a higher number of transactions to be processed within a given time frame.

3. Increased Maximum Supply

Litecoin deviated from Bitcoin's total supply by implementing a different issuance schedule. While Bitcoin has a maximum supply of 21 million coins, Litecoin's maximum supply is set at 84 million coins, four times that of Bitcoin. This decision aimed to strike a balance between providing a sufficient supply of coins while maintaining scarcity and preserving the store of value proposition. The increased maximum supply also allowed for a greater number of transactions to be accommodated as the network expanded.

4. Segregated Witness (SegWit) Implementation

In 2017, Litecoin became one of the early adopters of Segregated Witness (SegWit), a protocol upgrade that aimed to address scalability and transaction malleability issues. SegWit separated transaction signatures from the transaction data, resulting in more efficient use of block space and increased transaction capacity. The successful implementation of SegWit on Litecoin paved the way for its adoption on Bitcoin and other cryptocurrencies, contributing to the overall scalability and efficiency of the blockchain ecosystem.

5. Atomic Swaps and Lightning Network Integration

Litecoin has been at the forefront of pioneering technologies such as Atomic Swaps and Lightning Network integration. Atomic Swaps enable the trustless exchange of cryptocurrencies directly between different blockchains, eliminating the need for intermediaries. Litecoin's compatibility and collaboration with other cryptocurrencies through Atomic Swaps have expanded its utility and interoperability within the broader blockchain ecosystem. Additionally, Litecoin has actively explored Lightning Network integration, a layer-two scaling solution that enables faster and cheaper transactions by leveraging off-chain payment channels.

6. Continued Development and Innovation

Litecoin's technical features and advancements are not static but continue to evolve over time. The development team and community remain committed to ongoing innovation and improvements. Regular protocol upgrades, code optimizations, and the integration of new technologies are essential elements of Litecoin's development roadmap.

By staying at the forefront of technological advancements, Litecoin aims to remain a relevant and competitive cryptocurrency in the ever-changing landscape of digital finance.

Conclusion

Litecoin's technical features and advancements have played a crucial role in distinguishing it from Bitcoin and other cryptocurrencies. The adoption of the Scrypt hashing algorithm, faster block generation times, increased maximum supply, and innovations like SegWit, Atomic Swaps, and Lightning Network integration have positioned Litecoin as a versatile and forward-thinking digital currency. By prioritizing scalability, efficiency, and interoperability, Litecoin has expanded its use cases and contributed to the broader adoption and development of blockchain technology. As Litecoin continues to evolve, its technical innovations will continue to shape the future of the crypto industry.

Litecoin (LTC) emerged in 2011 as a prominent altcoin, introducing technical advancements and a unique positioning as "the silver to Bitcoin's gold." In this section, we delve into the market adoption and community development of Litecoin, exploring its journey from a nascent cryptocurrency to a well-established player in the digital finance landscape.

1. Early Adoption and Enthusiast Community

Litecoin garnered attention from early adopters and cryptocurrency enthusiasts who were intrigued by its vision as a complementary cryptocurrency to Bitcoin. The early community recognized Litecoin's potential for faster transaction confirmations and increased scalability, which made it well-suited for everyday use. These early adopters played a crucial role in spreading awareness, mining the currency, and contributing to its initial growth.

2. Exchange Listings and Market Presence

As Litecoin gained popularity, it started receiving listings on various cryptocurrency exchanges, making it more accessible to a broader audience. The availability of Litecoin on multiple platforms facilitated its trading and further contributed to its market adoption. The growing market presence of Litecoin also provided opportunities for individuals and businesses to use LTC for transactions, investments, and diversification within their crypto portfolios.

3. Merchant Acceptance and Use Cases

Merchant adoption played a significant role in shaping Litecoin's market adoption. An increasing number of merchants began accepting Litecoin as a payment method, recognizing its advantages over Bitcoin in terms of faster transaction confirmations and lower fees. This acceptance expanded the use cases for Litecoin, making it feasible for everyday purchases, e-commerce transactions, and even donations to charitable organizations. The availability of Litecoin payment processors and integrations further facilitated its adoption by businesses worldwide.

4. Community Engagement and Development

The Litecoin community has been an active and vibrant ecosystem, fostering development, collaboration, and innovation. The community has contributed to the growth of Litecoin through various initiatives, such as software development, improvement proposals, educational resources, and community-driven marketing efforts. Open communication channels, forums, social media groups, and meetups have allowed community members to connect, share knowledge, and build a strong support network around Litecoin.

5. Strategic Partnerships and Collaborations

Litecoin has formed strategic partnerships and collaborations with other blockchain projects, businesses, and organizations. These partnerships aim to enhance Litecoin's utility, interoperability, and adoption. Collaborations have included joint ventures, cross-chain compatibility initiatives, integration with payment processors, and co-marketing efforts. Such partnerships have not only strengthened Litecoin's position in the market but have also fostered synergies within the broader crypto ecosystem.

6. Developer Ecosystem and Innovation

The development of Litecoin has been driven by a dedicated team of developers and contributors who continually work on improving the protocol, implementing upgrades, and exploring new features. The open-source nature of Litecoin has encouraged developer participation and innovation. New technologies, integrations, and improvements, such as Segregated Witness (SegWit) implementation, Atomic Swaps, and Lightning Network support, have further expanded Litecoin's capabilities and positioned it as a pioneer in the crypto industry.

Conclusion

The market adoption and community development of Litecoin have played pivotal roles in establishing it as a leading cryptocurrency. From its early adoption by enthusiasts to its integration into merchant platforms and partnerships with other projects, Litecoin has proven its viability and utility in the digital finance ecosystem. The active community engagement, strategic collaborations, and constant innovation have solidified Litecoin's position as a trailblazer in the crypto landscape. As Litecoin continues to evolve, its market presence and community-driven initiatives will shape its future growth and impact within the realm of digital currencies.

Litecoin (LTC) has made a significant impact on the cryptocurrency ecosystem since its inception. As "the silver to Bitcoin's gold," Litecoin's unique features and market positioning have influenced various aspects of the crypto industry. This section explores the impact of Litecoin on the cryptocurrency ecosystem, including its influence on technological advancements, market dynamics, investor sentiment, and the broader adoption of cryptocurrencies.

1. Technological Advancements and Innovations

Litecoin's introduction of technical advancements has influenced the development and evolution of the cryptocurrency ecosystem as a whole. By adopting the Scrypt hashing algorithm, Litecoin demonstrated the feasibility of alternative hashing algorithms beyond Bitcoin's SHA-256. This diversification encouraged other projects to explore new algorithms, leading to increased innovation and resilience in the face of potential mining centralization. Additionally, Litecoin's implementation of Segregated Witness (SegWit) paved the way for its adoption on Bitcoin and other cryptocurrencies, addressing scalability issues and improving transaction efficiency across the industry.

2. Market Dynamics and Digital Asset Valuation

Litecoin's presence and performance have influenced market dynamics within the cryptocurrency ecosystem. As one of the earliest altcoins, Litecoin offered investors an alternative investment option to Bitcoin. Its unique positioning as a fast and scalable digital currency attracted attention and contributed to the growth of the overall crypto market. Litecoin's performance often serves as an indicator of investor sentiment and market trends. Significant price movements and trading volumes in Litecoin have ripple effects on other cryptocurrencies, impacting the valuation and perception of the entire digital asset space.

3. Blockchain Interoperability and Collaboration

Litecoin's collaborations and partnerships have fostered blockchain interoperability and collaboration within the cryptocurrency ecosystem. Through initiatives like Atomic Swaps, Litecoin has demonstrated the ability to exchange value seamlessly between different blockchains without the need for intermediaries. This breakthrough in cross-chain compatibility has inspired other projects to explore similar solutions, enhancing the interoperability of blockchain networks and paving the way for decentralized and trustless asset transfers. Litecoin's collaborations with other cryptocurrencies and projects have fostered a sense of unity, community-driven innovation, and the shared goal of advancing the broader blockchain ecosystem.

4. User Experience and Adoption

Litecoin's focus on faster block confirmations and lower transaction fees has improved the user experience for cryptocurrency transactions. By offering a more efficient alternative to Bitcoin for everyday use, Litecoin has contributed to the adoption of cryptocurrencies as a medium of exchange. Merchants and businesses have integrated Litecoin payment options, expanding its utility and acceptance in the real world. Litecoin's impact on user experience and adoption has paved the way for other cryptocurrencies to prioritize scalability, transaction speed, and cost-effectiveness.

5. Investor Education and Market Maturation

Litecoin's journey and its positioning as a prominent altcoin have played a role in educating investors and contributing to the maturation of the cryptocurrency market. Through Litecoin's development, investors have gained insights into different technical aspects, investment strategies, and risk management in the crypto space. The presence of Litecoin alongside Bitcoin has diversified investment portfolios, encouraging investors to explore beyond the dominant cryptocurrency. The lessons learned from Litecoin's market cycles and developments have contributed to a better understanding of market dynamics and improved decision-making for investors across the ecosystem.

6. Community Empowerment and Decentralization

Litecoin's community has played an essential role in the empowerment and decentralization of the cryptocurrency ecosystem. The active and engaged Litecoin community has fostered inclusivity, education, and decentralized decision-making processes. By supporting open-source development, community-driven marketing efforts, and grassroots initiatives, Litecoin has exemplified the power of decentralized communities in driving innovation, adoption, and awareness within the broader crypto space. The community-driven nature of Litecoin has inspired other projects to embrace similar principles, strengthening the decentralized ethos of the cryptocurrency ecosystem as a whole.

Conclusion

Litecoin's impact on the cryptocurrency ecosystem extends far beyond its status as an altcoin. Through its technological advancements, market influence, collaborations, and community engagement, Litecoin has shaped the development and maturation of the crypto industry. Its contributions in areas such as technological innovation, market dynamics, user experience, and community empowerment have had a lasting impact on the broader adoption and evolution of cryptocurrencies. As the cryptocurrency ecosystem continues to grow and evolve, Litecoin's influence will continue to be felt, propelling the industry forward with its commitment to innovation, decentralization, and the pursuit of a decentralized future.

The Concept of Sustainable and Energy-Efficient Cryptocurrency

Peercoin (PPC) stands out in the cryptocurrency landscape for its focus on sustainability and energy efficiency. In this section, we explore the concept of sustainable and energy-efficient cryptocurrency, as exemplified by Peercoin. We delve into the underlying principles, innovative mechanisms, and environmental considerations that shape Peercoin's approach to building a greener and more sustainable blockchain network.

1. The Environmental Impact of Traditional Proof-of-Work (PoW) Mechanisms

To understand the significance of sustainable and energy-efficient cryptocurrency, it is essential to examine the environmental impact of traditional PoW mechanisms. Bitcoin, the pioneering cryptocurrency, brought attention to the energy-intensive nature of PoW mining. The high computational power required for mining and securing the network has led to concerns about carbon emissions, energy consumption, and the long-term sustainability of such systems.

2. The Birth of Peercoin: A Sustainable Alternative

Peercoin emerged as an alternative to traditional PoW-based cryptocurrencies, with a specific focus on sustainability and energy efficiency. It introduced the concept of a hybrid PoW/PoS (Proof-of-Stake) consensus mechanism, combining the benefits of both approaches. Peercoin aimed to address the environmental concerns associated with PoW-based networks while maintaining security and decentralization.

3. Proof-of-Stake (PoS) and Energy Efficiency

The introduction of PoS in Peercoin's consensus mechanism significantly reduces the energy consumption compared to traditional PoW systems. PoS eliminates the need for resource-intensive mining hardware and replaces it with a system that allows participants to validate transactions and secure the network based on the number of coins they hold and are willing to "stake." This energy-efficient approach reduces the carbon footprint and fosters a more sustainable blockchain ecosystem.

4. The Importance of Energy Efficiency in Blockchain Networks

Energy efficiency in blockchain networks has become a critical consideration in the wake of increasing environmental concerns. Peercoin's commitment to energy efficiency not only mitigates the ecological impact but also contributes to long-term network stability. By designing a system that consumes less energy, Peercoin enhances the scalability and overall performance of the blockchain while minimizing the associated costs and environmental footprint.

5. Proof-of-Stake Minting and Security

Peercoin's hybrid PoW/PoS mechanism incorporates both mining and minting processes. Minting allows users to secure the network and earn rewards by holding and staking their Peercoin holdings. This approach reduces the reliance on resource-intensive mining hardware and empowers individual participants to contribute to the network's security and decentralization. Peercoin's unique minting process ensures the network's integrity while providing economic incentives for stakeholders.

6. The Economics of Sustainable Cryptocurrency

Sustainability in cryptocurrency extends beyond energy efficiency. Peercoin incorporates economic mechanisms that promote sustainability and long-term value preservation. Peercoin's deflationary design, which targets a 1% annual inflation rate, encourages coin holders to stake their holdings, reducing the circulating supply and maintaining scarcity. This economic model incentivizes participation, network security, and long-term value appreciation.

7. Environmental Considerations and Future Outlook

Peercoin's emphasis on sustainability and energy efficiency serves as a model for environmentally conscious blockchain networks. As the global focus on climate change intensifies, the demand for sustainable cryptocurrency solutions will likely increase. Peercoin's forward-thinking approach positions it as a leader in this space, providing valuable insights and solutions for building greener blockchain networks. Furthermore, Peercoin's approach can inspire other projects to prioritize sustainability and drive innovation in energy-efficient consensus mechanisms.

Conclusion

Peercoin's concept of sustainable and energy-efficient cryptocurrency highlights the importance of addressing environmental concerns within the blockchain ecosystem. By introducing a hybrid PoW/PoS consensus mechanism and promoting energy efficiency, Peercoin sets a precedent for building greener and more sustainable blockchain networks. Its approach not only reduces the carbon footprint but also enhances network security, scalability, and long-term value preservation. Peercoin's commitment to sustainability paves the way for future developments in environmentally conscious cryptocurrency systems, contributing to a more sustainable and eco-friendly future for the blockchain industry.

Peercoin (PPC) revolutionized the cryptocurrency landscape by introducing a hybrid consensus mechanism called Proof-of-Stake (PoS). In this section, we delve into the intricacies of the PoS hybrid model, exploring its principles, advantages, and impact on the sustainability and energy efficiency of Peercoin. By understanding the fundamentals of PoS, we can grasp how Peercoin achieves its vision of a greener and more sustainable blockchain network.

1. The Evolution of Consensus Mechanisms

Consensus mechanisms play a vital role in blockchain networks, ensuring agreement and validity among participants. Proof-of-Work (PoW) consensus, employed by Bitcoin and other early cryptocurrencies, relied on computational power and energy-intensive mining to secure the network. However, the emergence of PoS challenged the dominance of PoW by offering an alternative approach to achieving consensus.

2. Understanding Proof-of-Stake (PoS) Consensus

Proof-of-Stake (PoS) is a consensus mechanism that assigns the right to validate transactions and create new blocks based on participants' stake in the network. Instead of relying solely on computational power, PoS considers the ownership of coins or tokens held by participants. This ownership, or stake, determines their influence and ability to participate in the consensus process.

3. Hybridizing PoW and PoS: Peercoin's Approach

Peercoin introduced a hybrid model that combines both PoW and PoS elements, leveraging the strengths of each consensus mechanism. In the initial stages, PoW is used to mint new coins and secure the network. However, as the blockchain matures, the PoS component gains prominence, allowing participants to validate transactions and earn rewards based on the number of coins they hold and are willing to "stake." This hybrid approach ensures both network security and energy efficiency.

4. Advantages of the PoS Hybrid Model

The PoS hybrid model offers several advantages over traditional PoW or pure PoS consensus mechanisms. Firstly, it significantly reduces the energy consumption associated with mining, making it more environmentally friendly and sustainable. Secondly, it promotes decentralization by enabling broader participation and eliminating the need for specialized mining hardware. Additionally, the hybrid model provides a higher level of security against potential attacks, as it requires a majority stake to compromise the network.

5. Stakeholder Engagement and Network Governance

In a PoS hybrid model, stakeholders play a crucial role in network governance and decision-making. Participants with a stake in the network have the power to influence protocol changes, propose improvements, and vote on important network parameters. This stakeholder engagement fosters a sense of ownership and responsibility, aligning the interests of participants with the long-term success and stability of the blockchain.

6. Economic Incentives and Tokenomics

The PoS hybrid model introduces economic incentives to encourage participation and stakeholder engagement. By staking their tokens, participants earn rewards in the form of additional tokens, fostering network security and decentralization. Peercoin's unique economic model incorporates a deflationary design, aiming for a 1% annual inflation rate to maintain scarcity and incentivize token holders to stake their holdings. This economic framework ensures a sustainable token supply and enhances the long-term value of the cryptocurrency.

7. Scalability and Transaction Throughput

The PoS hybrid model addresses scalability concerns in blockchain networks. By reducing the reliance on resource-intensive mining, Peercoin improves transaction throughput and lowers confirmation times. The increased efficiency allows for more transactions to be processed, making Peercoin a viable solution for everyday transactions and facilitating broader adoption.

Conclusion

The introduction of the PoS hybrid model in Peercoin represents a significant milestone in the evolution of consensus mechanisms. By combining the strengths of PoW and PoS, Peercoin achieves a sustainable, energy-efficient cryptocurrency system. The PoS hybrid model offers environmental benefits, enhances decentralization, fosters stakeholder engagement, and improves scalability. Peercoin's innovative approach serves as a blueprint for other projects seeking to create greener, more efficient, and economically sustainable blockchain networks.

Peercoin (PPC) stands out among cryptocurrencies not only for its focus on sustainability and energy efficiency but also for its unique features and security enhancements. In this section, we explore the distinctive elements that set Peercoin apart from other digital currencies and examine how these features contribute to the overall security and resilience of the network. By understanding Peercoin's innovative approach, we gain insights into the advancements that have shaped its position as a trailblazer in the crypto space.

1. Energy Efficiency and Security Synergy

One of the key features of Peercoin is its ability to achieve energy efficiency without compromising network security. By incorporating the Proof-of-Stake (PoS) hybrid model, Peercoin reduces energy consumption while maintaining a robust security framework. We delve into the synergy between energy efficiency and security and how Peercoin leverages this unique combination to create a sustainable and secure cryptocurrency ecosystem.

2. Cold Minting: Enhancing Security and Accessibility

Peercoin introduces a feature called "cold minting" to enhance security and accessibility for stakeholders. Unlike traditional PoS systems that require participants to keep their wallets connected to the network to mint new coins, Peercoin's cold minting allows users to mint coins while their wallets remain offline. This offline minting process significantly reduces the risk of attacks and ensures the safety of participants' funds, making Peercoin an attractive option for long-term storage and security-conscious users.

3. Checkpointing: Protecting Against Blockchain Reorganizations

Blockchain reorganizations can pose a threat to the integrity of a cryptocurrency network. Peercoin addresses this concern through the implementation of a checkpointing mechanism. Checkpoints act as reference points in the blockchain, making it more difficult for attackers to rewrite transaction history and manipulate the network. This security enhancement provides additional protection against double-spending attacks and ensures the immutability of the Peercoin blockchain.

4. Enhanced Cold Minting with Hierarchical Deterministic (HD) Wallets

Peercoin leverages Hierarchical Deterministic (HD) wallets to enhance the security of cold minting. HD wallets generate a hierarchical structure of private and public keys, allowing users to generate an unlimited number of addresses without compromising the security of their private keys. This feature enables Peercoin users to create separate addresses for different purposes, such as minting, receiving payments, or managing funds, while maintaining a higher level of security and organizational control.

5. Resilience against 51% Attacks

51% attacks pose a significant threat to blockchain networks, enabling attackers to control the majority of the network's computing power. Peercoin implements security measures to mitigate the risk of such attacks. Through its PoS hybrid model, Peercoin requires a majority stake to compromise the network, making it economically and technically challenging for an attacker to gain control. This resilience against 51% attacks enhances the security and stability of the Peercoin network.

6. Active Development and Community Engagement

Peercoin's unique features and security enhancements are a result of active development and a vibrant community. The Peercoin development team continuously works on improving the protocol, introducing new features, and addressing any potential vulnerabilities. Additionally, the Peercoin community actively engages in discussions, feedback, and peer-reviewed research, ensuring the ongoing security and evolution of the network.

7. Third-Party Integrations and Collaboration

Peercoin's security enhancements and unique features have attracted the attention of third-party developers and organizations. The cryptocurrency has witnessed integrations with various platforms, wallets, and exchanges, expanding its ecosystem and reinforcing its security measures through collaboration. We explore notable partnerships and integrations that have contributed to the growth and security of the Peercoin network.

Conclusion

The unique features and security enhancements of Peercoin have established it as a prominent player in the cryptocurrency landscape. Through its energy-efficient PoS hybrid model, cold minting, checkpointing, HD wallets, and resilience against 51% attacks, Peercoin offers a secure and sustainable platform for digital transactions. The active development and engagement of the Peercoin community further solidify its position as a trailblazer in the crypto space.

Role in Shaping the Future of Blockchain Technology

Peercoin (PPC) has made significant contributions to the evolution of blockchain technology, particularly in terms of sustainability, energy efficiency, and security. In this section, we explore the role Peercoin plays in shaping the future of blockchain technology and its potential impact on the broader crypto ecosystem. By understanding the innovations and principles underlying Peercoin, we gain insights into its transformative potential and the implications for the future of decentralized finance.

1. Advancing Sustainability and Energy Efficiency

Peercoin's focus on sustainability and energy efficiency positions it as a pioneering force in the blockchain industry. By introducing the PoS hybrid model and energy-efficient consensus mechanisms, Peercoin addresses the growing concerns around the environmental impact of traditional PoW-based cryptocurrencies. We examine how Peercoin's sustainable approach sets a precedent for other projects and contributes to the overall sustainability of the crypto ecosystem.

2. Paving the Way for Energy-Efficient Blockchain Solutions

As the demand for blockchain technology continues to grow, energy consumption remains a significant challenge. Peercoin's success in achieving energy efficiency paves the way for the development of more sustainable blockchain solutions. We explore how Peercoin's principles and technological advancements inspire other projects to adopt energy-efficient approaches, ultimately driving the adoption of greener and more eco-friendly blockchain networks.

3. Influence on Proof-of-Stake (PoS) Implementation

Peercoin's introduction of the PoS hybrid model has had a profound influence on the broader adoption of PoS-based consensus mechanisms. We examine how Peercoin's successful implementation of PoS has inspired other projects to explore and adopt similar approaches. By shifting the focus from computational power to ownership stake, Peercoin has played a pivotal role in shaping the landscape of blockchain consensus mechanisms.

4. Encouraging Stakeholder Engagement and Governance

Peercoin's emphasis on stakeholder engagement and network governance sets a precedent for decentralized decision-making within blockchain networks. Through its PoS hybrid model, Peercoin empowers token holders to participate actively in network governance, consensus, and decision-making processes. We discuss how Peercoin's approach fosters community involvement and how this model can be applied to other blockchain projects to enhance decentralization and promote democratic governance.

5. Scalability and Transaction Throughput Advancements

Scalability has long been a concern in the blockchain industry, limiting the widespread adoption of cryptocurrencies for everyday transactions. Peercoin's focus on energy efficiency allows for increased transaction throughput and improved scalability. We examine Peercoin's contributions to addressing scalability challenges and how its advancements can shape the future of blockchain technology, making it more suitable for mass adoption and use cases beyond financial transactions.

6. Interoperability and Collaboration Potential

Peercoin's commitment to collaboration and integration positions it as a key player in fostering interoperability within the blockchain ecosystem. We explore Peercoin's potential to collaborate with other projects, protocols, and platforms to create synergies and unlock new possibilities. By working together, blockchain projects can leverage each other's strengths and accelerate the development of interoperable solutions, ultimately shaping a more connected and cohesive blockchain ecosystem.

7. Inspiring Sustainable Financial Systems

Beyond its technical contributions, Peercoin's vision of sustainability and energy efficiency inspires the development of sustainable financial systems. We discuss how Peercoin's principles align with the broader movement towards sustainable finance and the potential for decentralized finance (DeFi) applications to drive positive environmental and social change. Peercoin's approach serves as a blueprint for creating a more sustainable and inclusive financial landscape.

Conclusion

Peercoin's role in shaping the future of blockchain technology extends beyond its contributions to sustainability, energy efficiency, and security. By inspiring innovative consensus mechanisms, encouraging stakeholder engagement, addressing scalability challenges, fostering interoperability, and promoting sustainable financial systems, Peercoin sets a precedent for a more sustainable and inclusive blockchain ecosystem. Its principles and technological advancements have far-reaching implications for the future of decentralized finance and the broader adoption of blockchain technology.

Chapter 3: Bytecoin (BCN), established 2012 - "Private, untraceable cryptocurrency."

The Quest for Privacy: Untraceable Cryptocurrency

Bytecoin (BCN) emerged as a groundbreaking cryptocurrency with a primary focus on privacy and anonymity. In this section, we delve into the concept of untraceable cryptocurrency and explore how Bytecoin tackles the challenge of preserving user privacy. By understanding the underlying technology and innovative approaches employed by Bytecoin, we gain insights into the quest for privacy in the realm of digital currencies.

1. The Importance of Privacy in Digital Transactions

Privacy is a fundamental concern when it comes to financial transactions, both in traditional systems and the digital realm. We discuss the significance of privacy in digital transactions and the risks associated with the lack of privacy. Bytecoin's commitment to preserving privacy addresses these concerns and introduces a new paradigm in the cryptocurrency space.

2. Exploring the Cryptonote Protocol

Bytecoin's privacy features are built upon the Cryptonote protocol, which provides a solid foundation for untraceable transactions. We explore the key principles of the Cryptonote protocol, such as ring signatures and one-time addresses, that enable Bytecoin to achieve privacy and anonymity. By using ring signatures, Bytecoin obfuscates the transaction history, making it challenging to trace the flow of funds and link transactions to specific individuals.

3. Ring Signatures: Anonymity through Decoy Signers

Ring signatures form the core of Bytecoin's privacy framework. We delve into the concept of ring signatures, which allow a user to sign a transaction on behalf of a group, making it impossible to determine the actual signer. We explain how the use of decoy signers within the ring adds an extra layer of anonymity, making it extremely difficult to identify the true sender of a transaction. Bytecoin's implementation of ring signatures revolutionizes the concept of privacy in cryptocurrency transactions.

4. One-Time Addresses: Breaking the Linkability

Bytecoin's use of one-time addresses further enhances privacy by breaking the linkability between the sender and the recipient. We explore how one-time addresses are generated for each transaction, ensuring that the recipient's address cannot be associated with their identity or previous transactions. This feature adds an additional level of protection against blockchain analysis and enhances the privacy and anonymity of Bytecoin users.

5. Challenges and Innovations in Privacy Technology

The quest for privacy in cryptocurrencies is not without its challenges. We discuss the limitations and criticisms surrounding privacy-focused cryptocurrencies like Bytecoin, including issues related to regulatory compliance and potential misuse. However, we also highlight the innovations and advancements that Bytecoin and other privacy-focused projects are making to address these challenges. By continuously refining their privacy technologies, these projects strive to find a balance between privacy and responsible use.

6. Use Cases and Adoption of Bytecoin

Bytecoin's privacy features make it attractive for a range of use cases where anonymity is crucial. We explore the adoption of Bytecoin in various industries and applications, such as e-commerce, online marketplaces, and international transactions. By offering privacy-focused solutions, Bytecoin opens up opportunities for businesses and individuals to transact securely and confidentially.

7. Bytecoin and the Future of Privacy in Cryptocurrencies

Bytecoin's advancements in privacy technology have a broader impact on the future of cryptocurrencies. We discuss how Bytecoin's pioneering efforts have influenced the development of other privacy-focused cryptocurrencies and protocols. We also examine the potential for widespread adoption of privacy-centric cryptocurrencies as individuals and businesses recognize the value of preserving their financial privacy.

Conclusion

Bytecoin's untraceable and private nature has positioned it as a significant player in the cryptocurrency space. By implementing the Cryptonote protocol, utilizing ring signatures and one-time addresses, Bytecoin addresses the critical need for privacy in digital transactions. Its innovative approach to privacy technology contributes to the ongoing quest for confidentiality in the realm of digital currencies, setting the stage for a future where individuals can confidently and securely transact online while safeguarding their financial privacy.

Cryptonote Protocol and Ring Signatures

In this section, we delve into the underlying technology that powers Bytecoin's privacy features: the Cryptonote protocol and ring signatures. These innovative concepts form the foundation of Bytecoin's commitment to providing a private and untraceable cryptocurrency experience. By understanding how the Cryptonote protocol and ring signatures work together, we gain insights into the intricate mechanisms that make Bytecoin a pioneer in privacy-focused cryptocurrencies.

1. The Cryptonote Protocol: An Overview

The Cryptonote protocol serves as the backbone of Bytecoin's privacy features. We provide an overview of the Cryptonote protocol, explaining its fundamental principles and design philosophy. The protocol was developed to address the privacy limitations of earlier cryptocurrencies, paving the way for a new era of privacy-centric digital currencies.

2. Ring Signatures: Enabling Untraceable Transactions

Ring signatures play a crucial role in Bytecoin's privacy architecture. We dive deep into the concept of ring signatures, understanding how they enable untraceable transactions on the Bytecoin network. By examining the mathematics and cryptographic principles behind ring signatures, we uncover the mechanisms that make it nearly impossible to determine the true sender of a transaction.

3. Exploring the Construction of Ring Signatures

To grasp the inner workings of ring signatures, we explore their construction in detail. We explain how a ring signature is created using a group of possible signers, with the actual signer being hidden among the decoy signers. We delve into the mathematical calculations involved in generating and verifying ring signatures, shedding light on the robustness of this privacy-preserving mechanism.

4. Unraveling the Unlinkability of Ring Signatures

One of the key properties of ring signatures is their ability to break the linkability between a transaction and its actual signer. We delve into the unlinkability aspect of ring signatures, elucidating how they prevent outside observers from associating a transaction with a specific individual. By understanding the techniques used to achieve unlinkability, we appreciate the level of anonymity and privacy that Bytecoin offers.

5. Ring Signatures in Practice: Transaction Examples

To further illustrate the practical application of ring signatures, we provide real-world transaction examples on the Bytecoin network. By dissecting these transactions, we demonstrate how ring signatures are used to conceal the true sender, highlighting the effectiveness of this privacy-enhancing technology. These examples showcase the power of ring signatures in protecting the privacy of Bytecoin users.

6. Evaluating the Strengths and Limitations of Ring Signatures

While ring signatures offer a robust privacy solution, it is essential to evaluate their strengths and limitations. We explore the security aspects of ring signatures, including potential vulnerabilities and attack vectors. By understanding the potential risks associated with ring signatures, we gain a comprehensive view of the privacy assurances provided by Bytecoin's implementation of this technology.

7. The Evolution of Ring Signatures: From Bytecoin to Other Cryptocurrencies

The development of ring signatures in Bytecoin has had a significant impact on the broader cryptocurrency ecosystem. We discuss how Bytecoin's pioneering efforts in implementing ring signatures have influenced the development of other privacy-focused cryptocurrencies. We explore how other projects have adopted and adapted ring signatures, expanding the reach of this privacy-enhancing technology.

Conclusion

The Cryptonote protocol and ring signatures form the core of Bytecoin's privacy features. By employing these innovative technologies, Bytecoin has emerged as a trailblazer in the realm of private and untraceable cryptocurrencies. The robustness and effectiveness of ring signatures, coupled with the underlying principles of the Cryptonote protocol, provide users with a heightened level of privacy and confidentiality in their transactions. Bytecoin's commitment to privacy sets a precedent for the future of cryptocurrencies, where individuals can transact securely while maintaining their financial privacy.

Challenges and Innovations in Privacy Technology

In this section, we explore the challenges and innovations surrounding privacy technology in Bytecoin. While Bytecoin has made significant strides in providing a private and untraceable cryptocurrency, it has encountered various obstacles along the way. We delve into these challenges and examine the innovative solutions that Bytecoin and its community have implemented to enhance privacy technology.

1. The Importance of Privacy in the Digital Age:

We begin by highlighting the significance of privacy in the digital age, especially concerning financial transactions. With the increasing digitization of our lives, protecting personal and financial information has become a paramount concern. We discuss the implications of compromised privacy and the need for robust privacy technologies in cryptocurrencies like Bytecoin.

2. Identifying Privacy Challenges:

Next, we delve into the specific challenges faced by Bytecoin and other privacy-focused cryptocurrencies. We explore the technical and regulatory obstacles that hinder the achievement of complete privacy. These challenges include the traceability of transactions, privacy breaches, scalability concerns, and legal and regulatory compliance. We examine the impact of these challenges on the development and adoption of privacy technology in Bytecoin.

3. Innovations in Privacy Technology:

In response to the challenges, Bytecoin has introduced several innovative solutions to enhance privacy technology. We explore these innovations in depth, highlighting their significance in overcoming the obstacles faced by privacy-focused cryptocurrencies. Some of the key innovations we discuss include:

a. Stealth Addresses: We explain how Bytecoin employs stealth addresses to improve privacy. Stealth addresses enable the recipient's address to remain hidden on the blockchain, making it difficult for outside observers to associate transactions with specific individuals.

b. One-Time Ring Signatures: Bytecoin has introduced the concept of one-time ring signatures to address the potential risks associated with reusing ring signatures. We delve into how one-time ring signatures provide an extra layer of privacy by ensuring that each signature is unique and unlinkable.

c. Mixin Transactions: Bytecoin has implemented mixin transactions to enhance privacy and obfuscate the linkability of transactions. We explore how mixin transactions enable multiple inputs and outputs, making it challenging to trace the flow of funds.

d. Dynamic Fees: Bytecoin has implemented dynamic fees to improve privacy by eliminating transaction fee analysis. We discuss how dynamic fees help prevent transaction pattern recognition and enhance privacy protection.

e. Blockchain Analysis Resistance: Bytecoin has taken measures to enhance resistance against blockchain analysis techniques. We explore the strategies employed to minimize the effectiveness of analytical tools and techniques used to de-anonymize transactions.

4. Balancing Privacy and Compliance:

Achieving privacy in cryptocurrencies while complying with legal and regulatory requirements is a delicate balance. We examine how Bytecoin navigates this balance, ensuring privacy without enabling illicit activities. We discuss the challenges and implications of maintaining privacy in a regulatory landscape and how Bytecoin addresses these concerns.

5. Collaboration and Community Engagement:

The development of privacy technology in Bytecoin is a collaborative effort involving the broader community. We delve into the role of the community in identifying privacy challenges, proposing innovative solutions, and contributing to the ongoing development of privacy-enhancing features. We highlight the significance of community engagement in fostering a robust and sustainable privacy ecosystem.

6. Future Directions and Challenges:

As privacy technology evolves, new challenges and opportunities arise. We discuss the future directions and potential advancements in privacy technology for Bytecoin. We explore emerging technologies such as zero-knowledge proofs, secure multiparty computation, and confidential transactions that may further enhance privacy in Bytecoin and similar cryptocurrencies.

Conclusion:

Bytecoin's journey in providing a private and untraceable cryptocurrency has been marked by challenges and continuous innovation in privacy technology. By addressing these challenges and implementing innovative solutions, Bytecoin has positioned itself as a trailblazer in the realm of privacy-focused cryptocurrencies. As privacy becomes an increasingly critical aspect of digital transactions, Bytecoin's efforts shed light on the possibilities and limitations of privacy technology and its impact on the broader blockchain industry.

In this section, we explore the various use cases and adoption of Bytecoin, a private and untraceable cryptocurrency. We delve into the practical applications of Bytecoin and examine how its unique features and focus on privacy have attracted users and businesses alike. Additionally, we discuss the challenges and opportunities associated with the adoption of Bytecoin in different industries.

1. Secure and Private Transactions:

One of the primary use cases of Bytecoin lies in its ability to facilitate secure and private transactions. We explore how individuals and businesses leverage Bytecoin to conduct confidential transactions, protecting their financial privacy in an increasingly surveilled digital world. We discuss the benefits of private transactions and highlight specific industries that find value in the secure and untraceable nature of Bytecoin.

2. E-commerce and Online Marketplaces:

Bytecoin has gained adoption in the realm of e-commerce and online marketplaces. We delve into how Bytecoin provides a secure and private payment option for online merchants and consumers. We discuss the advantages of using Bytecoin in e-commerce, such as reduced transaction fees, fast settlement times, and protection against identity theft. Additionally, we explore notable e-commerce platforms and marketplaces that have integrated Bytecoin as a payment method.

3. Remittances and Cross-Border Payments:

The untraceable nature of Bytecoin makes it an attractive solution for remittances and cross-border payments. We examine how individuals and businesses use Bytecoin to send and receive funds across borders securely and anonymously. We discuss the challenges faced by traditional remittance services and explore how Bytecoin's decentralized and private infrastructure can address these challenges. Furthermore, we highlight real-world examples of individuals and organizations leveraging Bytecoin for cost-effective and efficient cross-border transactions.

4. Privacy-Conscious Individuals and Professionals:

Bytecoin has garnered attention from privacy-conscious individuals and professionals who value their financial privacy. We discuss how Bytecoin caters to these individuals, providing a reliable and private alternative to traditional financial systems. We explore specific professions and communities that have embraced Bytecoin, such as journalists, activists, whistleblowers, and individuals living in regions with limited financial privacy protections.

5. Gaming and Virtual Economies:

The gaming industry and virtual economies present unique use cases for cryptocurrencies like Bytecoin. We delve into how Bytecoin is utilized within gaming ecosystems, enabling secure and private transactions for in-game purchases, virtual assets, and decentralized marketplaces. We discuss the benefits of using Bytecoin in gaming, including the elimination of fraud, the ability to trade assets securely, and the promotion of user autonomy.

6. Adoption Challenges and Opportunities:

While Bytecoin has seen adoption in various sectors, it also faces challenges on the path to widespread acceptance. We discuss the hurdles encountered in terms of regulatory compliance, user education, and establishing trust among potential adopters. Additionally, we explore the opportunities for Bytecoin to expand its adoption through strategic partnerships, marketing initiatives, and community engagement.

7. Case Studies and Success Stories:

To provide concrete examples of Bytecoin adoption, we present case studies and success stories of individuals, businesses, or organizations that have integrated Bytecoin into their operations successfully. These case studies highlight the benefits and positive outcomes experienced by early adopters of Bytecoin, showcasing its practical value in real-world scenarios.

Conclusion:

Bytecoin's use cases and adoption reflect its role as a private and untraceable cryptocurrency. From facilitating secure transactions and powering e-commerce to addressing the needs of privacy-conscious individuals and professionals, Bytecoin has demonstrated its value in diverse industries. As adoption continues to grow, Bytecoin's impact on the financial landscape is set to expand, reshaping the way we perceive privacy and security in digital transactions.

Chapter 4: Monero (XMR), established 2014 - "Private, secure, and untraceable cryptocurrency." Introduction to Monero's Private, Secure, and Untraceable Design

In this section, we delve into the design principles that make Monero (XMR) a private, secure, and untraceable cryptocurrency. We explore the core features and technologies that differentiate Monero from other cryptocurrencies, highlighting its commitment to privacy and confidentiality. By understanding Monero's design, we gain insights into how it achieves anonymity and security for its users.

1. Anonymity and Fungibility:

Monero's primary goal is to provide users with complete anonymity and fungibility. We explore the concept of anonymity in cryptocurrencies, examining how Monero addresses the challenges faced by Bitcoin and other transparent blockchain-based systems. We discuss the importance of fungibility and how Monero ensures that each unit of XMR is indistinguishable from another, thereby preserving its value as a medium of exchange.

2. Ring Signatures:

One of the fundamental technologies employed by Monero is ring signatures. We explain how ring signatures allow for transaction obfuscation by mixing the spender's transaction with multiple decoy inputs, making it nearly impossible to trace the origin of funds. We delve into the mechanics of ring signatures and discuss their role in achieving privacy and unlinkability in Monero transactions.

3. Stealth Addresses:

Monero utilizes stealth addresses to enhance user privacy and protect the recipient's identity. We explore how stealth addresses work by generating unique one-time addresses for each transaction, ensuring that the recipient's actual address remains hidden. We discuss the advantages of stealth addresses, such as preventing address reuse and making it difficult for third parties to track transaction history.

4. Ring Confidential Transactions (RingCT):

To address the issue of transaction amounts being visible on the blockchain, Monero incorporates Ring Confidential Transactions (RingCT). We explain how RingCT allows for confidential transactions by hiding the transaction amount while still ensuring the validity of the transaction. We discuss the cryptographic mechanisms behind RingCT and its role in achieving privacy and confidentiality in Monero transactions.

5. Kovri and I2P Integration:

Monero places a strong emphasis on network-level privacy by integrating with the Kovri project, which leverages the Invisible Internet Project (I2P). We explore how Kovri enhances Monero's privacy by encrypting and routing network traffic through a decentralized and anonymous overlay network. We discuss the benefits of Kovri integration, such as IP address obfuscation and resistance against network surveillance.

6. Dandelion++ and Bulletproofs:

Monero continually evolves to enhance its privacy and efficiency. We discuss the recent advancements in Monero, including the implementation of the Dandelion++ protocol for transaction broadcasting, which further obscures the origin of transactions. Additionally, we explore the integration of Bulletproofs, a zero-knowledge proof technology that reduces transaction size and improves scalability without compromising privacy.

7. Privacy Trade-Offs and Limitations:

While Monero strives to be a leader in privacy-focused cryptocurrencies, there are trade-offs and limitations to consider. We discuss the challenges faced by Monero, such as potential regulatory scrutiny and usability concerns related to the complexity of privacy features. We also explore the ongoing research and development efforts within the

Monero community to address these limitations and enhance the overall privacy and usability of the network.

Conclusion:

Monero's private, secure, and untraceable design sets it apart as a leading cryptocurrency for users seeking enhanced financial privacy. By employing technologies such as ring signatures, stealth addresses, RingCT, Kovri integration, and ongoing improvements like Dandelion++ and Bulletproofs, Monero has established itself as a trailblazer in the realm of privacy-focused cryptocurrencies. The principles and technologies underlying Monero's design provide a strong foundation for users to transact with confidence and maintain their financial sovereignty in an increasingly interconnected world.

Ring Confidential Transactions (RingCT) and Stealth Addresses

In this section, we delve into the advanced privacy features of Monero (XMR), namely Ring Confidential Transactions (RingCT) and Stealth Addresses. These technologies play a pivotal role in ensuring the confidentiality and untraceability of transactions within the Monero network. We explore how RingCT and Stealth Addresses enhance the privacy of Monero transactions, making it nearly impossible to link the sender, receiver, and transaction amounts.

1. The Need for Enhanced Transaction Privacy:

We begin by discussing the limitations of transparent blockchain systems like Bitcoin in terms of transaction privacy. We highlight the importance of obfuscating transaction details, including the sender, receiver, and amount, to protect user privacy and maintain fungibility. We then introduce RingCT and Stealth Addresses as the key privacy-enhancing technologies in Monero.

2. Understanding Ring Confidential Transactions (RingCT):

Ring Confidential Transactions (RingCT) is a cryptographic protocol employed by Monero to hide transaction amounts. We explain the mathematical foundations of RingCT, including commitments, range proofs, and the use of Pedersen commitments. We explore how RingCT allows Monero users to obfuscate transaction amounts while still ensuring that the transaction is valid and the sums balance.

3. Ring Signatures in RingCT:

Ring Signatures, a technology we previously discussed in the context of Monero's privacy features, are also utilized within RingCT. We revisit the concept of ring signatures and explain how they are applied within RingCT to ensure the anonymity of the sender. We explore the mechanics of ring signatures in RingCT and discuss how they contribute to transaction privacy.

4. Advantages and Benefits of RingCT:

We delve into the advantages and benefits that RingCT brings to the Monero ecosystem. We discuss how RingCT addresses the issue of transaction amount visibility, making it significantly more challenging to link transactions and determine the exact amounts being transferred. We highlight the role of RingCT in enhancing fungibility, privacy, and confidentiality within the Monero network.

5. Stealth Addresses and Address Privacy:

Stealth Addresses are another critical component of Monero's privacy architecture. We explore how Stealth

Addresses work by generating unique one-time addresses for each transaction, thereby concealing the receiver's actual address. We discuss the advantages of Stealth Addresses in preventing address reuse, improving transaction privacy, and making it difficult for external observers to link multiple transactions to the same recipient.

6. Sender and Receiver Privacy:

We delve deeper into how RingCT and Stealth Addresses contribute to the overall privacy of Monero transactions by protecting the identities of both the sender and the receiver. We discuss how the sender's identity is obfuscated through ring signatures and the use of decoy inputs, while the receiver's identity remains hidden through the generation of unique one-time Stealth Addresses.

7. Assessing the Effectiveness of RingCT and Stealth Addresses:

We evaluate the effectiveness of RingCT and Stealth Addresses in achieving transaction privacy within the Monero network. We discuss real-world examples and case studies that demonstrate the challenges faced by external observers in attempting to trace Monero transactions and link them to specific participants. We also address potential attack vectors and the ongoing efforts within the Monero community to continually improve the privacy features.

Conclusion:

Ring Confidential Transactions (RingCT) and Stealth Addresses are instrumental in making Monero a private, secure, and untraceable cryptocurrency. These technologies provide a robust framework for protecting the privacy of transactions and maintaining the fungibility of Monero (XMR). By combining ring signatures, RingCT, and Stealth Addresses, Monero achieves a high level of transaction privacy that is unmatched in many other blockchain systems. The implementation of these advanced privacy features underscores Monero's commitment to providing individuals with a financial tool that prioritizes confidentiality and user sovereignty.

The Battle Against Blockchain Analysis

In this section, we explore the ongoing battle between Monero (XMR) and blockchain analysis. As a private, secure, and untraceable cryptocurrency, Monero has become a target for those seeking to uncover transaction details and trace user identities. We delve into the techniques employed by blockchain analysts, the challenges they face when analyzing Monero transactions, and the countermeasures implemented by the Monero community to preserve transaction privacy.

1. Understanding Blockchain Analysis:

We provide an overview of blockchain analysis, its goals, and its methods. We explain how blockchain analysts attempt to trace transactions, identify participants, and uncover patterns of activity within public blockchains. We discuss the tools and techniques used by analysts, such as address clustering, transaction graph analysis, and heuristics to deanonymize blockchain transactions.

2. Anonymity Challenges in Public Blockchains:

We highlight the inherent challenges of achieving anonymity in public blockchains like Bitcoin. We discuss the pseudonymous nature of blockchain transactions and how certain features, such as address reuse and transparent transaction histories, can compromise user privacy. We emphasize the need for enhanced privacy solutions like Monero to address these challenges.

3. Monero's Privacy Technology vs. Blockchain Analysis:

We delve into the privacy technologies employed by Monero, such as ring signatures, Ring Confidential Transactions (RingCT), and Stealth Addresses, and explain how they counteract the efforts of blockchain analysts. We discuss how ring signatures obfuscate the sender's identity, RingCT hides transaction amounts, and Stealth Addresses protect the receiver's identity. We explore the cryptographic principles and mathematical foundations behind these technologies.

4. The Challenges Faced by Blockchain Analysts:

We examine the specific challenges faced by blockchain analysts when attempting to analyze Monero transactions. We discuss the impact of ring signatures, RingCT, and Stealth Addresses on the traceability of transactions and the identification of participants. We explore the limitations of address clustering and transaction graph analysis techniques in the context of Monero's privacy features.

5. Transaction Linkability and Untraceability:

We delve into the concept of transaction linkability in Monero and how it presents a significant obstacle for blockchain analysts. We explain how Monero's privacy features break the transaction graph, making it extremely difficult to establish links between transactions and track the flow of funds. We discuss decoy inputs, mixins, and the obfuscation of transaction histories as key factors in achieving transaction untraceability.

6. Countermeasures and Improvements:

We discuss the proactive measures taken by the Monero community to stay ahead in the battle against blockchain analysis. We explore ongoing research and development efforts to further enhance Monero's privacy features, such as advancements in RingCT, implementation of Bulletproofs, and the exploration of alternative privacy-enhancing technologies like Kovri and Triptych. We highlight the collaborative nature of the Monero community and its commitment to preserving transaction privacy.

7. The Cat and Mouse Game Continues:

We conclude by acknowledging that the battle against blockchain analysis is an ongoing process. As blockchain analysis techniques evolve, the Monero community must remain vigilant and continually innovate to maintain transaction privacy. We emphasize the importance of education and user awareness in utilizing Monero's privacy features effectively and thwarting the efforts of those seeking to breach transaction privacy.

Conclusion:

The battle against blockchain analysis represents a fundamental aspect of Monero's mission to provide private, secure, and untraceable transactions. Through the implementation of advanced privacy technologies and ongoing community efforts, Monero continues to challenge the capabilities of blockchain analysts and maintain its position as one of the most privacy-focused cryptocurrencies in existence.

In this section, we explore the real-world applications and market positioning of Monero (XMR), a private, secure, and untraceable cryptocurrency. We delve into the industries and use cases where Monero has gained traction, its unique value proposition in the market, and the challenges and opportunities it faces as it strives for wider adoption.

1. Monero's Value Proposition:

We begin by discussing Monero's value proposition and its unique selling points. We explore how its emphasis on privacy, security, and untraceability differentiates it from other cryptocurrencies. We highlight the importance of financial privacy in an increasingly digital world and explain how Monero addresses the need for confidential transactions.

2. Privacy in E-Commerce:

We examine the role of Monero in e-commerce and its potential to enhance privacy in online transactions. We discuss the drawbacks of traditional payment systems in terms of privacy and security, and how Monero can provide a more confidential alternative. We explore the potential benefits of using Monero for online purchases, including protecting sensitive financial information and reducing the risk of identity theft.

3. Confidentiality in Peer-to-Peer Transactions:

We explore the applications of Monero in peer-to-peer transactions, such as person-to-person payments or remittances. We discuss how Monero's privacy features can enable individuals to conduct transactions without the fear of their financial activities being exposed. We highlight the potential use cases in countries with unstable economies, where privacy and protection from government surveillance are crucial.

4. Privacy for Business Transactions:

We delve into the role of Monero in business transactions and its potential benefits for commercial use cases. We discuss how Monero's privacy features can protect sensitive financial information and trade secrets in business-to-business transactions. We explore the challenges faced by businesses in maintaining confidentiality and how Monero can address those concerns.

5. Non-Profit Organizations and Donations:

We explore the applications of Monero in the realm of non-profit organizations and donations. We discuss the importance of privacy and anonymity in charitable giving and how Monero can facilitate transparent yet confidential transactions. We highlight the potential for increased trust and donor participation in the non-profit sector through the use of Monero.

6. Challenges and Regulatory Considerations:

We address the challenges and regulatory considerations associated with Monero's real-world applications. We discuss the concerns raised by governments and regulatory bodies regarding the potential misuse of privacy-focused cryptocurrencies. We explore the need for striking a balance between privacy and compliance, and how Monero can navigate these challenges to gain wider acceptance.

7. Market Positioning and Adoption:

We analyze Monero's current market positioning and adoption rates. We examine its position among other cryptocurrencies in terms of market capitalization, trading volume, and community support. We explore the factors that contribute to Monero's success, such as its active development community, strong brand identity, and growing ecosystem of supporting services and platforms.

8. Future Outlook and Potential:

We conclude by discussing the future outlook and potential for Monero. We highlight the ongoing development efforts, research, and community engagement that contribute to its growth. We explore the potential for partnerships, integrations, and increased adoption in various industries. We also address the challenges Monero may face in achieving mainstream recognition and the steps being taken to overcome them.

Conclusion:

Monero's real-world applications and market positioning are crucial factors in its journey towards becoming a widely adopted private, secure, and untraceable cryptocurrency. By providing privacy-enhancing features and addressing the needs of various industries, Monero offers a viable alternative for individuals and businesses seeking confidential transactions in the digital realm.

Chapter 5: Zcash (ZEC), established 2016 - "Privacy-protecting digital currency."

Exploring Zcash's Privacy-Protecting Features

In this section, we delve into the privacy-protecting features of Zcash (ZEC), a groundbreaking cryptocurrency that prioritizes confidentiality. We explore the technological innovations behind Zcash's privacy protocols and the mechanisms it employs to enable secure and private transactions. By understanding Zcash's privacy features, we gain insight into the importance of privacy in the digital currency landscape and its potential applications in various industries.

1. The Need for Privacy in Cryptocurrency:

We begin by discussing the need for privacy in the cryptocurrency space. We highlight the challenges associated with transparent transactions and the lack of anonymity in traditional cryptocurrencies like Bitcoin. We explore the implications of financial privacy and the growing demand for confidential transactions in an increasingly digital and interconnected world.

2. Zero-Knowledge Proofs and zk-SNARKs:

We explore the core privacy technology behind Zcash: zero-knowledge proofs and zk-SNARKs (Zero-Knowledge Succinct Non-Interactive Argument of Knowledge). We explain the cryptographic principles and mathematical concepts that underpin these privacy-enhancing protocols. We highlight how zero-knowledge proofs allow users to prove the validity of a transaction without revealing sensitive information.

3. Private and Transparent Transactions:

We delve into Zcash's dual transaction model, which allows users to choose between private (shielded) transactions and transparent (unshielded) transactions. We explain the differences between these two transaction types and their implications for privacy and traceability. We discuss the benefits and considerations associated with each approach, providing real-world examples of use cases where privacy is of utmost importance.

4. Shielded Pools and Addresses:

We explore the concept of shielded pools and addresses in Zcash. We explain how shielded pools aggregate transactions to enhance privacy and make it more challenging to trace individual transactions. We discuss the advantages and limitations of shielded pools and addresses and their impact on the overall privacy ecosystem of Zcash.

5. Selective Disclosure and Auditability:

We discuss the selective disclosure feature of Zcash, which allows users to reveal specific transaction details while still maintaining overall privacy. We explain how this feature enables compliance with regulatory requirements and facilitates auditing without compromising user privacy. We explore the potential use cases where selective disclosure can play a vital role in business transactions and financial services.

6. Integration and Interoperability:

We delve into the integration and interoperability aspects of Zcash. We discuss the challenges and opportunities of integrating Zcash's privacy features into existing cryptocurrency exchanges, wallets, and financial platforms. We explore the collaborations and partnerships that have enabled Zcash to expand its reach and foster interoperability with other blockchain networks.

7. Limitations and Future Enhancements:

We address the limitations of Zcash's privacy-protecting features and discuss ongoing efforts to enhance the protocol. We explore the challenges associated with scalability, transaction speed, and the balance between privacy and regulatory compliance. We highlight the research and development initiatives aimed at addressing these limitations and improving the overall privacy ecosystem of Zcash.

8. Potential Applications:

We explore the potential applications of Zcash's privacy-protecting features across different industries. We discuss how Zcash can be used in financial services, healthcare, supply chain management, and other sectors that require confidential transactions and data privacy. We highlight the benefits that Zcash can bring to these industries and the potential for transformative change through the adoption of privacy-protecting digital currencies.

Conclusion:

Zcash's privacy-protecting features offer a unique proposition in the digital currency landscape. By leveraging zero-knowledge proofs and zk-SNARKs, Zcash enables secure, private, and confidential transactions. The exploration of Zcash's privacy-protecting features provides insights into the significance of privacy in cryptocurrencies and its potential impact on various industries. Understanding Zcash's technological advancements paves the way for envisioning a future where privacy is a fundamental aspect of digital transactions.

In this section, we delve into the technological foundations of Zcash (ZEC) and its privacy-protecting features. We explore the concept of zero-knowledge proofs and their implementation through zk-SNARKs (Zero-Knowledge Succinct Non-Interactive Argument of Knowledge). By understanding the principles behind these cryptographic protocols, we gain insight into the powerful privacy-enhancing capabilities of Zcash.

1. The Need for Privacy in Cryptocurrencies:

We begin by discussing the importance of privacy in the context of cryptocurrencies. We explore the challenges associated with transparency in traditional cryptocurrencies like Bitcoin and the implications for user privacy. We delve into the motivations behind the development of privacy-protecting digital currencies and the role they play in addressing these privacy concerns.

2. Understanding Zero-Knowledge Proofs:

We introduce the concept of zero-knowledge proofs, a cryptographic technique that allows one party (the prover) to prove the knowledge of certain information to another party (the verifier) without revealing any additional information. We explain the principles behind zero-knowledge proofs, including soundness, completeness, and zero-knowledge property. We discuss the different types of zero-knowledge proofs and their applications beyond cryptocurrencies.

3. Introduction to zk-SNARKs:

We explore zk-SNARKs (Zero-Knowledge Succinct Non-Interactive Argument of Knowledge), the specific type of zero-knowledge proof used in Zcash. We explain the mechanics of zk-SNARKs, including the process of generating and verifying proofs. We discuss the computational efficiency and succinctness of zk-SNARKs, which enable Zcash to maintain privacy without compromising scalability.

4. Shielding Transactions with zk-SNARKs:

We delve into how zk-SNARKs are employed in Zcash to shield transactions and protect user privacy. We explain the process of creating shielded transactions, which involve generating zk-SNARK proofs to demonstrate transaction validity without revealing sensitive information. We discuss the cryptographic primitives and algorithms used in Zcash's implementation of zk-SNARKs.

5. Trade-offs and Challenges:

We address the trade-offs and challenges associated with the use of zk-SNARKs in Zcash. We discuss the computational requirements and time-consuming nature of generating and verifying zk-SNARK proofs. We explore the considerations in terms of hardware requirements, network scalability, and potential limitations when dealing with large-scale transaction volumes.

6. Privacy and Soundness Guarantees:

We examine the privacy and soundness guarantees provided by zk-SNARKs in Zcash. We discuss the mathematical foundations and cryptographic assumptions that ensure the confidentiality of shielded transactions. We explore the role of zero-knowledge proofs in preventing double-spending and ensuring the integrity of the Zcash network.

7. Ongoing Research and Improvements:

We highlight the ongoing research and development efforts in the field of zero-knowledge proofs and zk-SNARKs. We discuss the potential improvements and optimizations that can enhance the efficiency and scalability of zk-SNARKs, making them more accessible to a wider range of applications.

8. Beyond Zcash: Applications of Zero-Knowledge Proofs:

We explore the broader applications of zero-knowledge proofs beyond Zcash. We discuss how zero-knowledge proofs are being used in other domains such as identity verification, authentication, and data privacy. We highlight the potential for zero-knowledge proofs to revolutionize various industries by enabling secure and private transactions without compromising sensitive information.

Conclusion:

The implementation of zero-knowledge proofs and zk-SNARKs in Zcash revolutionizes the concept of privacy in digital currencies. By leveraging these cryptographic protocols, Zcash provides users with the ability to transact privately while maintaining the integrity of the blockchain. The exploration of zero-knowledge proofs and zk-SNARKs in this chapter reveals the innovative advancements that Zcash brings to the realm of privacy-protecting digital currencies and sets the stage for further developments in the field of cryptographic privacy.

Achievements and Challenges in Privacy-Preserving Technology

In this section, we explore the achievements and challenges associated with privacy-preserving technology in the context of Zcash (ZEC). We delve into the accomplishments of Zcash in revolutionizing privacy in digital currencies and discuss the ongoing challenges that exist in this evolving landscape. By understanding both the achievements and the hurdles, we gain a comprehensive view of the state of privacy-preserving technology and its implications for the future.

1. Advancements in Privacy Technology:

We begin by highlighting the significant achievements of Zcash in advancing privacy technology. We discuss the groundbreaking introduction of zk-SNARKs (Zero-Knowledge Succinct Non-Interactive Argument of Knowledge) and their impact on privacy within the cryptocurrency space. We explore how Zcash has set a precedent for other privacy-focused projects and sparked innovation in the field of privacy-preserving technology.

2. Enhanced User Privacy:

We delve into the ways in which Zcash enhances user privacy compared to traditional transparent cryptocurrencies. We discuss the ability to conduct shielded transactions, which provide a high level of privacy and confidentiality. We highlight the importance of protecting user identities and transaction details in preserving financial autonomy and security.

3. Resisting Blockchain Analysis:

We examine Zcash's effectiveness in resisting blockchain analysis, which is crucial for maintaining privacy. We discuss the role of zero-knowledge proofs and zk-SNARKs in obscuring transaction information, making it challenging for external observers to link transactions and identify the parties involved. We explore the implications of this resistance to blockchain analysis for user privacy and security.

4. Adoption and Integration:

We assess the adoption and integration of Zcash within the cryptocurrency ecosystem. We explore the partnerships, collaborations, and exchanges that support Zcash, providing users with the ability to transact and store value privately. We discuss the challenges and opportunities associated with widespread adoption and the integration of privacy-preserving cryptocurrencies into existing financial systems.

5. Regulatory and Legal Challenges:

We address the regulatory and legal challenges faced by privacy-focused cryptocurrencies like Zcash. We examine the tension between privacy and compliance with anti-money laundering (AML) and know-your-customer (KYC) regulations. We explore the evolving landscape of cryptocurrency regulations and discuss the potential impact on privacy-preserving technologies.

6. Scalability and Efficiency:

We discuss the scalability and efficiency challenges associated with privacy-preserving technologies like Zcash. We explore the computational requirements of zero-knowledge proofs and zk-SNARKs, which can impose limitations on transaction speed and network scalability. We highlight ongoing research and development efforts to address these challenges and improve the efficiency of privacy-preserving technologies.

7. Usability and User Experience:

We examine the usability and user experience aspects of privacy-preserving technologies. We discuss the user interface and user-friendly tools that have been developed to facilitate the adoption and usage of privacy-focused cryptocurrencies like Zcash. We explore the challenges of striking a balance between privacy and convenience, ensuring that privacy-preserving technologies are accessible to a broad user base.

8. Future Directions and Innovations:

We explore the future directions and potential innovations in privacy-preserving technology. We discuss the emerging advancements in cryptographic protocols, privacy-enhancing technologies, and consensus mechanisms that could further enhance privacy and scalability. We also consider the role of interoperability and collaboration between different privacy-focused projects.

Conclusion:

The achievements and challenges in privacy-preserving technology showcased by Zcash illustrate the transformative power of privacy in the realm of digital currencies. While significant strides have been made, there are still hurdles to overcome to achieve widespread adoption and usability. By addressing these challenges, privacy-preserving technologies can revolutionize the way we transact and interact in the digital world, empowering individuals with control over their financial privacy and security.

In this section, we delve into the adoption and future potential of Zcash (ZEC) as a privacy-protecting digital currency. We explore the current state of adoption, the challenges faced by Zcash in gaining widespread acceptance, and the potential future developments that could drive its growth and impact in the cryptocurrency ecosystem.

1. Current Adoption Landscape:

We start by examining the current adoption landscape of Zcash. We analyze its market presence, liquidity, and trading volume across various cryptocurrency exchanges. We discuss the geographical distribution of Zcash users and the industries or sectors that have shown interest in adopting Zcash for privacy-enhanced transactions. We also explore the use cases where Zcash has gained traction and its positioning relative to other privacy-focused cryptocurrencies.

2. User Base and Community:

We explore the user base and community that have embraced Zcash. We discuss the demographics, motivations, and values of Zcash users, including individuals, businesses, and organizations. We highlight the role of the Zcash community in supporting development, fostering innovation, and promoting adoption. We also examine the engagement and participation of the community in governance and decision-making processes.

3. Partnerships and Integrations:

We delve into the partnerships and integrations that Zcash has established with other players in the cryptocurrency and financial industries. We discuss collaborations with exchanges, wallets, payment processors, and other infrastructure providers that facilitate the use of Zcash. We explore the strategic alliances and initiatives aimed at expanding Zcash's reach and accessibility to a broader user base.

4. Regulatory Considerations:

We address the regulatory considerations and challenges that impact the adoption of Zcash. We discuss the evolving regulatory landscape surrounding privacy-focused cryptocurrencies and the potential impact on Zcash's adoption. We explore compliance with anti-money laundering (AML) and know-your-customer (KYC) regulations, as well as the implications of privacy-enhancing features for regulatory compliance.

5. Challenges and Barriers:

We analyze the challenges and barriers that Zcash faces in achieving widespread adoption. We discuss technological limitations, scalability concerns, user experience hurdles, and the complexities associated with privacy-enhancing technologies. We also address the perception and reputation challenges that privacy-focused cryptocurrencies may encounter and the need for education and awareness to overcome these barriers.

6. Future Development Roadmap:

We explore the future development roadmap of Zcash and the potential enhancements and innovations that could drive its future adoption. We discuss upcoming protocol upgrades, improvements in usability, scalability solutions, and research advancements in privacy-preserving technologies. We also examine the governance model of Zcash and its implications for decision-making and long-term sustainability.

7. Integration with Financial Systems:

We analyze the potential integration of Zcash with existing financial systems and institutions. We discuss the opportunities and challenges associated with bridging the gap between privacy-focused cryptocurrencies and traditional financial infrastructure. We explore partnerships with banks, payment processors, and fintech companies that can facilitate the seamless integration of Zcash into mainstream financial services.

8. Future Potential and Impact:

We assess the future potential and impact of Zcash on the broader cryptocurrency ecosystem and the financial industry as a whole. We discuss the disruptive nature of privacy-enhancing technologies and the potential role of Zcash in reshaping financial privacy, security, and censorship resistance. We also explore potential use cases and sectors where Zcash could find significant adoption and create transformative change.

Conclusion:

The adoption and future potential of Zcash are crucial factors in understanding its role as a privacy-protecting digital currency. By analyzing the current landscape, addressing challenges, and exploring future developments, we gain insights into the trajectory of Zcash and its potential impact on the way we transact and preserve privacy in the digital age.

Chapter 6: Comparative Analysis and Synergies Contrasting the Unique Attributes of the Featured Coins

In this section, we compare and contrast the unique attributes of the featured coins—Litecoin (LTC), Peercoin (PPC), Bytecoin (BCN), Monero (XMR), and Zcash (ZEC). We delve into their respective strengths, weaknesses, and innovative features that set them apart in the cryptocurrency landscape. By understanding their distinct characteristics, we gain insights into the diverse approaches and philosophies that drive the development of these cryptocurrencies.

1. Speed and Scalability:

We examine the speed and scalability aspects of each coin. We analyze their transaction processing times, block confirmation times, and their ability to handle a high volume of transactions. We explore the underlying technology and consensus mechanisms that contribute to their speed and scalability, highlighting any notable achievements or limitations.

2. Privacy and Anonymity:

We compare the privacy and anonymity features offered by each coin. We discuss their approaches to obfuscating transaction details, protecting user identities, and ensuring fungibility. We explore the different privacy technologies employed, such as ring signatures, zk-SNARKs, and the Cryptonote protocol. We also evaluate the level of privacy achieved and the trade-offs associated with each approach.

3. Security and Resistance to Attacks:

We assess the security measures implemented by each coin to safeguard against potential attacks. We discuss the consensus algorithms and cryptographic techniques utilized to ensure the integrity of the blockchain. We analyze their resilience to known vulnerabilities, such as 51% attacks and double-spending attempts. We also explore any innovative security enhancements unique to each coin.

4. Energy Efficiency and Sustainability:

We examine the energy efficiency and sustainability aspects of the featured coins. We discuss the energy consumption associated with their consensus mechanisms, comparing the environmental impact of proof-of-work (PoW) and proof-of-stake (PoS) models. We analyze any initiatives or innovations aimed at reducing energy consumption and promoting sustainable practices.

5. Governance and Decentralization:

We explore the governance models adopted by the featured coins and their approaches to decentralization. We discuss the decision-making processes, community involvement, and mechanisms for protocol upgrades and improvements. We evaluate the level of decentralization achieved and the potential implications for security, scalability, and long-term sustainability.

6. Use Cases and Adoption:

We examine the use cases and adoption of each coin in real-world scenarios. We discuss the industries or sectors where they have found practical applications and gained traction. We analyze their market positioning, user base, and the level of acceptance by merchants and businesses. We also explore any partnerships or integrations that have contributed to their adoption.

7. Synergies and Collaborations:

We explore the potential synergies and collaborations between the featured coins. We discuss any ongoing efforts to foster interoperability, cross-chain transactions, or shared research initiatives. We analyze the potential benefits of collaboration in addressing common challenges and advancing the development of privacy-enhancing technologies.

8. Future Outlook:

We provide a glimpse into the future outlook of the featured coins. We discuss the challenges they may face and the potential opportunities for growth and innovation. We explore how their unique attributes can contribute to the broader cryptocurrency ecosystem and shape the future of privacy, security, and decentralized finance.

Conclusion:

By contrasting the unique attributes of the featured coins, we gain a comprehensive understanding of their strengths, weaknesses, and the innovative approaches they bring to the table. Each coin offers a distinct set of features and philosophies, catering to different needs and preferences within the cryptocurrency community. Understanding these differences allows us to appreciate the diverse ecosystem and the potential synergies that can be leveraged to drive further innovation and adoption.

In this section, we explore the potential synergies and collaborations within the cryptocurrency ecosystem, focusing on Zcash (ZEC) and its interactions with other prominent cryptocurrencies. By identifying areas of collaboration, we can uncover opportunities for innovation, interoperability, and shared advancements. We delve into the possibilities of cross-chain integrations, research initiatives, and partnerships that can enhance the overall development and adoption of privacy-focused digital currencies.

1. Interoperability and Cross-Chain Transactions:

We discuss the importance of interoperability within the crypto ecosystem and how it can facilitate seamless transactions and asset transfers between different blockchains. We examine the potential for Zcash to collaborate with other cryptocurrencies to enable cross-chain functionality, allowing users to transact and exchange assets across multiple networks. We explore existing interoperability projects and their implications for privacy-focused cryptocurrencies.

2. Research Collaborations:

We delve into the realm of research collaborations between Zcash and other cryptocurrencies. We explore the possibilities of shared research initiatives focused on privacy-enhancing technologies, cryptography, and blockchain scalability. We discuss the potential benefits of pooling resources, expertise, and insights to drive innovation and solve common challenges faced by privacy-centric cryptocurrencies.

3. Privacy-Focused Partnerships:

We analyze potential partnerships between Zcash and other privacy-focused cryptocurrencies. We explore the synergies that can be created by combining the strengths of different platforms to provide enhanced privacy features and user experiences. We discuss the potential for joint development efforts, integrations, or strategic alliances to further strengthen privacy solutions within the crypto ecosystem.

4. Exchange Listings and Liquidity:

We examine the importance of exchange listings and liquidity for cryptocurrencies, including Zcash. We discuss potential collaborations with cryptocurrency exchanges to ensure widespread availability and accessibility of Zcash tokens. We explore the benefits of liquidity partnerships, market-making initiatives, and the integration of Zcash into decentralized finance (DeFi) platforms to enhance token utility and liquidity.

5. Regulatory Compliance and Industry Initiatives:

We delve into the regulatory landscape and industry initiatives that can benefit Zcash and other privacy-focused cryptocurrencies. We discuss collaborations with regulatory bodies and industry associations to ensure compliance with legal requirements and promote responsible usage of privacy-enhancing technologies. We explore the potential for self-regulatory frameworks and industry-wide standards to foster trust and adoption.

6. Privacy Infrastructure Development:

We explore collaborations in the development of privacy infrastructure within the crypto ecosystem. We discuss the potential for joint efforts to enhance privacy solutions, such as the development of privacy-focused wallets, decentralized exchanges, or privacy-focused smart contract platforms. We analyze the benefits of shared expertise and resources in advancing the state-of-the-art in privacy technology.

7. Community Collaboration and Governance:

We discuss the importance of community collaboration and governance in the crypto ecosystem. We explore the potential for collaboration between Zcash and other cryptocurrencies to engage their respective communities, promote transparency, and foster decentralized decision-making processes. We discuss the benefits of sharing best practices, community-driven initiatives, and the potential for cross-project collaboration.

8. Future Synergies and Collaborations:

We provide insights into the potential future synergies and collaborations within the crypto ecosystem, focusing on Zcash and its interactions with other privacy-focused cryptocurrencies. We discuss emerging trends, technological advancements, and regulatory developments that can shape the landscape of collaboration. We explore the potential for increased integration, standardization, and shared initiatives to drive the adoption and acceptance of privacy-focused digital currencies.

Conclusion:

By identifying synergies and collaborations within the crypto ecosystem, we unlock opportunities for innovation, interoperability, and shared advancements. Zcash, along with other privacy-focused cryptocurrencies, can benefit from strategic partnerships, research collaborations, regulatory compliance initiatives, and community-driven efforts. These collaborations pave the way for enhanced privacy solutions, improved user experiences, and increased adoption of privacy-protecting digital currencies. As the crypto ecosystem evolves, the potential for collaboration will continue to shape the future of privacy, security, and decentralized finance.

Lessons Learned and Impact on the Broader Blockchain Industry

In this section, we reflect on the lessons learned from the development and adoption of Zcash (ZEC) and its impact on the broader blockchain industry. We examine the technological innovations, privacy enhancements, and community-driven initiatives that have shaped Zcash's journey. Furthermore, we analyze the implications of Zcash's experiences and achievements on the overall blockchain ecosystem, including privacy standards, regulatory considerations, and the evolution of decentralized finance (DeFi) applications.

1. Privacy as a Fundamental Right:

We discuss the fundamental importance of privacy in the context of blockchain technology. We explore how Zcash's focus on privacy has highlighted the need for robust privacy solutions within the blockchain industry. We examine the impact of Zcash's innovations on the broader understanding of privacy as a fundamental right, leading to increased awareness and demand for privacy-enhancing technologies in the crypto space.

2. Technological Advancements:

We delve into the technological advancements pioneered by Zcash and their impact on the broader blockchain industry. We discuss Zcash's introduction of zk-SNARKs (zero-knowledge succinct non-interactive arguments of knowledge) and their application in achieving privacy and confidentiality in transactions. We analyze how Zcash's technological breakthroughs have influenced the development of privacy protocols and inspired other projects to explore similar solutions.

3. Evolving Regulatory Landscape:

We examine the impact of Zcash on the regulatory landscape surrounding privacy-focused cryptocurrencies. We discuss the challenges and considerations faced by Zcash in terms of regulatory compliance and the balance between privacy and transparency. We explore how Zcash's experiences have shaped regulatory discussions and influenced the development of frameworks and guidelines for privacy-preserving digital assets.

4. Advancing Privacy Standards:

We analyze how Zcash's emphasis on privacy has driven the development of privacy standards within the blockchain industry. We explore the establishment of best practices and protocols for privacy protection in cryptocurrencies, including the adoption of zero-knowledge proofs, ring signatures, and other privacy-enhancing technologies. We discuss how Zcash's efforts have raised the bar for privacy standards and influenced the development of privacy-focused projects.

5. Impact on Decentralized Finance (DeFi):

We discuss the impact of Zcash on the evolution of decentralized finance (DeFi) applications. We explore the integration of Zcash into DeFi protocols, such as lending platforms, decentralized exchanges, and privacy-focused smart contract platforms. We analyze how Zcash's privacy features have enabled new use cases and expanded the possibilities for privacy-centric DeFi applications.

6. User Adoption and Community Growth:

We examine the impact of Zcash's user adoption and community growth on the broader blockchain industry. We discuss how Zcash's focus on privacy has attracted a dedicated user base and fostered a vibrant community of developers, contributors, and enthusiasts. We explore the lessons learned from community-driven governance models and the impact of strong community engagement on the sustainability and success of blockchain projects.

7. Education and Awareness:

We discuss the role of Zcash in raising awareness and educating the broader blockchain community about the importance of privacy. We explore Zcash's initiatives in promoting privacy education, privacy-centric tools, and user-friendly interfaces. We examine the impact of Zcash's educational efforts in fostering a privacy-conscious mindset among blockchain participants and driving the adoption of privacy-preserving technologies.

8. Collaborative Ecosystem:

We analyze the collaborative ecosystem that has emerged around Zcash and its impact on the broader blockchain industry. We discuss partnerships, research collaborations, and joint initiatives that have been formed to advance privacy technology and interoperability. We examine the lessons learned from successful collaborations and the potential for cross-project synergies to drive innovation and accelerate the development of privacy-focused solutions.

Conclusion:

The journey of Zcash has provided valuable insights and lessons for the broader blockchain industry. Its focus on privacy, technological advancements, regulatory considerations, and community-driven initiatives have reshaped the landscape of privacy-preserving digital currencies. The impact of Zcash's experiences extends beyond its own network, influencing privacy standards, regulatory discussions, and the development of decentralized finance applications. As the blockchain industry continues to evolve, the lessons learned from Zcash will serve as a guiding light for the future of privacy, security, and user-centric innovation in the digital age.

Chapter 7: The Future of PoW and Beyond
Evaluating the Role of PoW in the Ever-Changing Crypto Landscape

In this section, we delve into the role of Proof-of-Work (PoW) in the ever-changing crypto landscape. We examine the strengths and weaknesses of PoW consensus mechanisms and evaluate their relevance in the face of emerging technologies, scalability challenges, and environmental concerns. Furthermore, we explore alternative consensus mechanisms and their potential to reshape the future of blockchain technology.

1. Understanding Proof-of-Work (PoW):

We provide a comprehensive overview of the Proof-of-Work consensus mechanism, its underlying principles, and its historical significance in the development of cryptocurrencies. We discuss the role of PoW in achieving consensus, securing the network, and preventing double-spending attacks. We analyze the computational puzzle-solving process involved in PoW and its impact on network security and decentralization.

2. Scalability Challenges:

We examine the scalability challenges associated with PoW consensus mechanisms. We discuss the limitations of PoW in terms of transaction throughput, block confirmation times, and network congestion. We explore the implications of these challenges on the usability and adoption of PoW-based cryptocurrencies, and the need for innovative solutions to address scalability concerns.

3. Environmental Impact:

We evaluate the environmental impact of PoW consensus mechanisms, particularly in the context of increasing energy consumption and carbon footprint. We discuss the criticisms surrounding the energy-intensive nature of PoW and its potential implications for sustainability and climate change. We examine the ongoing efforts to develop energy-efficient alternatives and the potential trade-offs between security, decentralization, and environmental sustainability.

4. PoW vs. Alternative Consensus Mechanisms:

We compare PoW with alternative consensus mechanisms, such as Proof-of-Stake (PoS), Delegated Proof-of-Stake (DPoS), and Byzantine Fault Tolerance (BFT). We evaluate the strengths and weaknesses of these mechanisms in terms of scalability, energy efficiency, security, and decentralization. We explore real-world examples of cryptocurrencies that have adopted alternative consensus models and discuss their implications for the future of blockchain technology.

5. Innovations in PoW:

We discuss the innovations and advancements within the PoW ecosystem aimed at addressing its limitations. We explore concepts such as sharding, off-chain scaling solutions, and hybrid consensus models that combine the benefits of PoW with other consensus mechanisms. We analyze the potential of these innovations to improve scalability, energy efficiency, and overall network performance.

6. Evolutionary Paths for PoW:

We examine the potential evolutionary paths for PoW in response to emerging technologies and industry demands. We discuss the concept of "greener" PoW, where energy-efficient mining methods and renewable energy sources are utilized to mitigate environmental impact. We explore the integration of PoW with layer 2 solutions and interoperability protocols to enhance scalability and improve transaction speeds. We also examine the potential for PoW to coexist and collaborate with other consensus mechanisms in hybrid models.

7. The Importance of Community Consensus:

We emphasize the significance of community consensus in shaping the future of PoW and the broader crypto landscape. We discuss the role of governance, community-driven initiatives, and open-source development in guiding the evolution of PoW. We explore the challenges and opportunities associated with achieving consensus among stakeholders and the potential impact on network upgrades, protocol changes, and the overall direction of PoW-based cryptocurrencies.

Conclusion:

The role of Proof-of-Work (PoW) in the ever-changing crypto landscape is a topic of ongoing discussion and exploration. While PoW has been the foundation of many successful cryptocurrencies, it faces challenges in scalability and environmental sustainability. As the industry evolves, alternative consensus mechanisms and innovative approaches to PoW are being explored to address these concerns. The future of PoW will be shaped by technological advancements, community consensus, and the need to balance security, scalability, and sustainability. By critically evaluating the role of PoW and considering alternative models, we can lay the foundation for a more efficient, inclusive, and sustainable blockchain ecosystem.

In this section, we explore the emerging trends and technologies that are shaping the future of Proof-of-Work (PoW) and the broader crypto landscape. We delve into innovative solutions, advancements in blockchain technology, and the potential impact of these developments on the evolution of PoW consensus mechanisms. By analyzing these emerging trends, we gain insights into the direction of the industry and the opportunities that lie ahead.

1. Layer 2 Scaling Solutions:

We discuss the emergence of layer 2 scaling solutions as a response to the scalability challenges faced by PoW-based cryptocurrencies. We delve into technologies such as payment channels, state channels, and sidechains that enable off-chain transactions and reduce the burden on the main blockchain. We explore the benefits of layer 2 solutions in terms of increased transaction throughput, reduced fees, and improved scalability.

2. Interoperability Protocols:

We examine the rise of interoperability protocols that enable seamless communication and exchange of assets between different blockchains. We discuss the importance of interoperability in fostering collaboration, expanding use cases, and enhancing liquidity across multiple blockchain networks. We explore technologies such as cross-chain bridges, atomic swaps, and interoperability-focused blockchains that facilitate interoperability between PoW-based cryptocurrencies and other blockchain platforms.

3. Quantum Computing and Post-Quantum Cryptography:

We explore the potential impact of quantum computing on the security of PoW-based cryptocurrencies. We discuss the unique threat that quantum computers pose to cryptographic algorithms used in blockchain networks. We delve into the development of post-quantum cryptography and its potential to provide robust security in the era of quantum computing. We examine the ongoing research and efforts to implement post-quantum cryptographic algorithms in PoW-based cryptocurrencies.

4. Decentralized Finance (DeFi):

We analyze the rise of decentralized finance (DeFi) and its implications for PoW-based cryptocurrencies. We discuss the emergence of decentralized exchanges, lending platforms, stablecoins, and other financial applications built on blockchain technology. We explore the potential of DeFi to disrupt traditional financial systems, increase financial inclusion, and provide new avenues for investment and wealth creation.

5. Governance and Decentralized Autonomous Organizations (DAOs):

We examine the growing importance of governance and decentralized autonomous organizations (DAOs) in shaping the future of PoW-based cryptocurrencies. We discuss the role of on-chain governance mechanisms, token voting systems, and community-driven decision-making processes. We explore the potential of DAOs to foster decentralized governance, enhance transparency, and ensure the alignment of incentives among network participants.

6. Privacy and Confidentiality Enhancements:

We delve into the advancements in privacy and confidentiality technologies within PoW-based cryptocurrencies. We discuss the development of zero-knowledge proofs, confidential transactions, and privacy-focused protocols that aim to enhance the privacy features of blockchain networks. We explore the potential applications of these technologies in areas such as financial transactions, supply chain management, and identity verification.

7. Sustainable Mining Practices:

We address the growing concerns about the environmental impact of PoW-based cryptocurrencies and the emergence of sustainable mining practices. We discuss the exploration of alternative energy sources, the utilization of renewable energy for mining operations, and the development of energy-efficient mining hardware. We examine the potential of sustainable mining practices to mitigate the environmental footprint of PoW-based cryptocurrencies.

Conclusion:

The future of Proof-of-Work (PoW) and the broader crypto landscape is being shaped by emerging trends and technologies. Layer 2 scaling solutions, interoperability protocols, quantum-resistant cryptography, DeFi, governance mechanisms, privacy enhancements, and sustainable mining practices are among the key areas driving innovation and evolution. By embracing these emerging trends, the industry can unlock new possibilities, improve scalability, security, and privacy, and pave the way for the next phase of blockchain technology adoption.

Speculating on the Future of Blockchain and Cryptocurrencies

In this section, we embark on a speculative journey to explore the potential future of blockchain technology and cryptocurrencies beyond the realm of Proof-of-Work (PoW). While we cannot predict the exact course of development, we can examine emerging trends, ongoing research, and expert opinions to speculate on the possibilities that lie ahead. This exploration allows us to envision a future where blockchain and cryptocurrencies have a transformative impact on various industries and society as a whole.

1. Scalability and Mass Adoption:

We speculate on the scalability challenges that blockchain technology must overcome to achieve mass adoption. We discuss the potential solutions being explored, such as sharding, state channels, and layer 2 scaling solutions. We delve into the possibility of blockchain networks achieving transaction speeds comparable to traditional payment systems and supporting a massive number of users without sacrificing security or decentralization.

2. Interoperability and Cross-Chain Communication:

We speculate on the evolution of interoperability protocols and cross-chain communication. We envision a future where different blockchain networks seamlessly interact, allowing for the transfer of assets and data across platforms. We discuss the potential emergence of a universal interoperability standard that enables efficient collaboration between various blockchain ecosystems.

3. Governance and Decentralized Decision-Making:

We delve into the potential for further advancements in blockchain governance and decentralized decision-making. We speculate on the development of more sophisticated on-chain governance models and the emergence of decentralized autonomous organizations (DAOs) with increased autonomy and self-sustainability. We explore the possibility of blockchain networks becoming self-regulating and enabling community-driven decision-making processes.

4. Enhanced Privacy and Confidentiality:

We discuss the future of privacy and confidentiality in blockchain technology. We speculate on the continued development of advanced cryptographic techniques, such as zero-knowledge proofs and homomorphic encryption, to ensure robust privacy features. We envision a future where individuals have full control over their personal data while still participating in transparent and verifiable transactions.

5. Integration with Emerging Technologies:

We explore the potential synergies between blockchain technology and other emerging technologies. We speculate on the integration of blockchain with artificial intelligence (AI), the Internet of Things (IoT), and decentralized machine learning. We discuss the possibilities of blockchain-based smart contracts interacting with AI algorithms and IoT devices to create autonomous and efficient systems.

6. Tokenization of Real-World Assets:

We speculate on the tokenization of real-world assets, including properties, commodities, and intellectual property rights. We envision a future where assets can be represented as digital tokens on blockchain networks, allowing for fractional ownership, increased liquidity, and efficient transfer of value. We discuss the potential impact of asset tokenization on traditional financial systems and the democratization of investment opportunities.

7. Regulation and Institutional Adoption:

We explore the future of regulation and institutional adoption of cryptocurrencies and blockchain technology. We speculate on the development of clear regulatory frameworks that balance innovation and consumer protection. We discuss the potential entry of institutional players, such as banks and governments, into the blockchain space and the impact of their involvement on mainstream adoption.

Conclusion:

While our speculation on the future of blockchain and cryptocurrencies is based on current trends and ongoing research, it is important to acknowledge that the future is inherently uncertain. However, by examining emerging technologies, scalability solutions, governance models, privacy enhancements, integration with other technologies, asset tokenization, and regulatory developments, we can paint a broad picture of the potential transformative impact of blockchain technology and cryptocurrencies in the years to come. It is a future that holds great promise for decentralized, secure, and transparent systems that empower individuals and reshape industries.

Conclusion

Recapitulating the Journey of PoW Trailblazers

As we conclude our exploration of Proof-of-Work (PoW) trailblazers in the cryptocurrency space, it is important to recapitulate the remarkable journey we have undertaken. Throughout this study, we have examined the evolution, technical features, market adoption, and impact of PoW-based cryptocurrencies such as Bitcoin, Litecoin, Peercoin, Bytecoin, Monero, and Zcash. We have delved into their unique attributes, challenges, and contributions to the broader blockchain industry. In this final section, we summarize the key findings and reflect on the significance of their accomplishments.

1. Bitcoin: Pioneering the Way

We reflect on the groundbreaking creation of Bitcoin by the anonymous figure known as Satoshi Nakamoto. Bitcoin introduced the world to the concept of decentralized digital currency and established the foundation for subsequent PoW-based cryptocurrencies. We highlight its role as a store of value, medium of exchange, and catalyst for innovation in the financial ecosystem. We acknowledge Bitcoin's role in inspiring the development of numerous altcoins and shaping the trajectory of the entire cryptocurrency market.

2. Litecoin: The Silver to Bitcoin's Gold

We recapitulate the emergence of Litecoin as a complementary cryptocurrency to Bitcoin. Litecoin's focus on faster transaction confirmation times and a different hashing algorithm aimed to address some of the limitations of Bitcoin. We recognize Litecoin's contributions to the development of the cryptocurrency ecosystem, including the adoption of Segregated Witness (SegWit) and the implementation of the Lightning Network. We emphasize Litecoin's position as a valuable alternative to Bitcoin and its ongoing relevance in the market.

3. Peercoin: Sustainability and Energy Efficiency

We summarize the innovative approach of Peercoin in introducing the concept of a hybrid PoW and Proof-of-Stake (PoS) consensus mechanism. Peercoin aimed to address the energy consumption and scalability concerns associated with pure PoW cryptocurrencies. We highlight the significance of Peercoin's sustainability and energy efficiency, as well as its influence on subsequent PoS-based cryptocurrencies. We acknowledge Peercoin's role in promoting a greener and more sustainable blockchain ecosystem.

4. Bytecoin: Untraceable Privacy

We reflect on the quest for privacy in the cryptocurrency space, exemplified by Bytecoin. We recapitulate the introduction of the Cryptonote protocol and ring signatures, which enabled untraceable transactions and enhanced privacy features. We recognize Bytecoin's role as a pioneer in privacy-centric cryptocurrencies and its impact on the development of subsequent privacy-focused projects.

5. Monero: Private, Secure, and Untraceable

We summarize the advancements made by Monero in achieving enhanced privacy, security, and untraceability. We emphasize the introduction of technologies such as Ring Confidential Transactions (RingCT) and Stealth Addresses, which have contributed to Monero's position as one of the leading privacy-oriented cryptocurrencies. We acknowledge Monero's commitment to maintaining a strong focus on privacy and its ongoing efforts to combat blockchain analysis.

6. Zcash: Privacy-Protecting Digital Currency

We recapitulate the introduction of Zcash as a privacy-protecting digital currency. We highlight the unique features of Zcash, including the utilization of zero-knowledge proofs and zk-SNARKs, which enable private transactions while still allowing for selective transparency. We recognize Zcash's contribution to the advancement of privacy technology in the cryptocurrency space and its potential for real-world applications where privacy is of utmost importance.

Conclusion:

In conclusion, the journey of PoW trailblazers has been characterized by innovation, challenges, and paradigm-shifting advancements in the blockchain industry. Bitcoin paved the way for decentralized digital currencies, while subsequent PoW-based cryptocurrencies such as Litecoin, Peercoin, Bytecoin, Monero, and Zcash have introduced unique features and addressed specific concerns within the cryptocurrency ecosystem.

Through our exploration, we have witnessed the evolution of PoW-based cryptocurrencies from their early beginnings to their current status as influential players in the digital financial landscape. These cryptocurrencies have demonstrated the potential of blockchain technology to disrupt traditional financial systems, empower individuals, and provide new avenues for innovation.

While each cryptocurrency has its own strengths and focuses, they collectively contribute to the broader blockchain industry's growth and evolution. The lessons learned from their successes, challenges, and innovations have paved the way for further advancements in scalability, privacy, energy efficiency, governance, and interoperability.

As we conclude our study, it is essential to recognize the ongoing nature of the cryptocurrency journey. The field of blockchain technology is continuously evolving, and new trailblazers will emerge, pushing the boundaries of what is possible. The impact of PoW-based cryptocurrencies will continue to shape the future of finance, governance, privacy, and numerous other sectors.

As we bid farewell to our exploration of PoW trailblazers, we eagerly anticipate the next chapter in the evolution of cryptocurrencies, where new ideas, technologies, and collaborations will propel the industry forward into uncharted territories. The journey continues, and the possibilities are endless.

Reflections on the Transformative Power of Early Cryptocurrencies

In this concluding section, we reflect on the transformative power of early cryptocurrencies and their profound impact on the financial landscape. Throughout our exploration of Bitcoin, Litecoin, Peercoin, Bytecoin, Monero, and Zcash, we have witnessed the emergence of decentralized digital currencies that challenge traditional financial systems, empower individuals, and pave the way for a more inclusive and secure future. In this final segment, we delve into the key reflections and insights gained from studying these groundbreaking cryptocurrencies.

1. Disruption of Traditional Finance:

One of the most significant reflections on early cryptocurrencies is their disruptive potential in traditional finance. Bitcoin, as the first decentralized digital currency, opened the door to a new paradigm of trustless peer-to-peer transactions, removing the need for intermediaries and enabling financial sovereignty for individuals. The subsequent cryptocurrencies built upon this foundation, offering unique features and addressing specific challenges to further disrupt the financial landscape.

2. Empowerment and Financial Inclusion:

Early cryptocurrencies have played a vital role in empowering individuals around the world, particularly those who lack access to traditional banking services. Cryptocurrencies provide a means for financial inclusion, enabling anyone with internet access to participate in the global economy. By removing geographical barriers and reducing transaction costs, cryptocurrencies have the potential to empower individuals in underserved regions and unlock economic opportunities.

3. Innovation in Blockchain Technology:

The development of early cryptocurrencies has sparked a wave of innovation in blockchain technology. Bitcoin introduced the concept of distributed ledger technology, and subsequent cryptocurrencies have built upon its foundations to explore new possibilities. From the introduction of Proof-of-Stake (PoS) consensus mechanisms to the advancements in privacy-enhancing technologies, these cryptocurrencies have contributed to the maturation and diversification of blockchain technology.

4. Challenges and Lessons Learned:

Reflection on early cryptocurrencies also entails acknowledging the challenges and lessons learned throughout their evolution. Scalability, energy consumption, regulatory concerns, and usability are among the hurdles faced by these cryptocurrencies. However, these challenges have driven innovation and prompted the exploration of alternative solutions. The lessons learned from early cryptocurrencies have informed the development of subsequent projects, allowing for continuous improvement and adaptation.

5. Societal Implications:

The transformative power of early cryptocurrencies extends beyond the realm of finance. Cryptocurrencies have sparked discussions on topics such as decentralization, privacy, governance, and the democratization of information. These technologies have the potential to redefine power structures, challenge existing norms, and enable individuals to take control of their digital identities. As society grapples with the implications of cryptocurrencies, it is crucial to foster dialogue and explore the potential benefits and risks they present.

6. Collaboration and Synergies:

An essential reflection on early cryptocurrencies is the significance of collaboration and synergies within the crypto ecosystem. While each cryptocurrency has its unique features and objectives, the industry's advancement relies on collaboration, knowledge sharing, and collective efforts. Collaboration between projects, developers, researchers, and the wider community fosters innovation, drives standardization, and ensures the sustainable growth of the ecosystem.

Conclusion:

In conclusion, the transformative power of early cryptocurrencies is undeniable. Bitcoin's emergence as the first decentralized digital currency paved the way for subsequent cryptocurrencies that have challenged traditional finance, empowered individuals, and pushed the boundaries of technological innovation. Reflections on these early cryptocurrencies highlight their disruptive potential, the importance of financial inclusion, the lessons learned from challenges faced, the societal implications they raise, and the need for collaboration within the crypto ecosystem.

As we move forward, it is crucial to leverage the insights gained from the evolution of early cryptocurrencies to address the remaining challenges, foster responsible innovation, and build a more inclusive and sustainable financial ecosystem. The journey of cryptocurrencies is far from over, and as technology continues to advance, it is our collective responsibility to ensure that the transformative power of cryptocurrencies is harnessed for the betterment of society.

Through our exploration of these trailblazing cryptocurrencies, we have gained a deeper understanding of their impact and potential. It is now up to us, as individuals, developers, researchers, and policymakers, to seize the opportunities presented by these technologies and shape a future where financial sovereignty, privacy, and inclusivity are at the forefront.

The transformative power of early cryptocurrencies has only just begun to unfold. As we embark on the next phase of this digital revolution, we must remain committed to the principles that underpin this movement: decentralization, transparency, security, and empowerment. By doing so, we can collectively shape a future where cryptocurrencies and blockchain technology contribute to a more equitable and prosperous world.

In this concluding section, we explore the opportunities and challenges that lie ahead in the blockchain space. As we reflect on the transformative power of cryptocurrencies and the evolution of blockchain technology, it becomes evident that the journey is far from over. In this segment, we delve into the potential opportunities and the significant challenges that need to be addressed as we navigate the future of blockchain.

1. Opportunities in Decentralized Finance (DeFi):

Decentralized Finance, or DeFi, has emerged as one of the most promising areas within the blockchain space. DeFi platforms enable users to access financial services without relying on intermediaries, offering opportunities for seamless cross-border transactions, transparent lending and borrowing, and innovative investment mechanisms. The growth of DeFi presents a transformative opportunity to democratize access to financial services and reshape the traditional financial landscape.

2. Blockchain Interoperability and Scalability:

One of the key challenges facing blockchain technology is interoperability and scalability. As the number of blockchain networks and applications continues to grow, the need for seamless interoperability becomes increasingly important. Interoperability solutions, such as cross-chain protocols and interoperability frameworks, hold immense potential to connect disparate blockchain networks and enable smooth data and asset transfers. Additionally, addressing scalability issues through improved consensus mechanisms, layer-two solutions, and sharding techniques is crucial for blockchain technology to reach mainstream adoption.

3. Enhancing Privacy and Security:

Privacy and security remain critical challenges in the blockchain space. While privacy-enhancing technologies have made significant strides, there is still room for improvement. Innovations such as zero-knowledge proofs, ring signatures, and secure multi-party computation can further enhance user privacy and confidentiality. Additionally, addressing security vulnerabilities, smart contract audits, and implementing robust governance frameworks are essential to ensure the security of blockchain networks and protect user assets.

4. Sustainable and Energy-Efficient Solutions:

The environmental impact of blockchain technology, particularly proof-of-work (PoW) consensus mechanisms, has been a topic of concern. As the industry matures, there is a growing need for sustainable and energy-efficient solutions. Transitioning to alternative consensus mechanisms like proof-of-stake (PoS), where energy consumption is significantly lower, and exploring innovative approaches such as energy-efficient consensus algorithms and green blockchain initiatives can pave the way for a greener blockchain ecosystem.

5. Regulatory and Legal Frameworks:

Regulatory clarity and the establishment of legal frameworks are vital for the widespread adoption of blockchain technology. As governments and regulatory bodies strive to understand and regulate the crypto landscape, striking the right balance between innovation and consumer protection becomes crucial. Collaborative efforts between industry participants, policymakers, and regulators are necessary to create favorable regulatory environments that foster innovation while ensuring compliance, investor protection, and consumer rights.

6. Education and Awareness:

Education and awareness play a pivotal role in unlocking the full potential of blockchain technology. As the technology becomes more complex, it is essential to educate individuals, businesses, and policymakers about its benefits, use cases, and potential risks. Promoting blockchain literacy, providing educational resources, and encouraging research and development initiatives will empower stakeholders to make informed decisions and drive adoption across various industries.

Conclusion:

Looking ahead, the blockchain space presents both opportunities and challenges. Embracing decentralized finance, enhancing interoperability and scalability, improving privacy and security, promoting sustainability, establishing regulatory frameworks, and fostering education and awareness are key areas to focus on. Collaboration between industry players, governments, academia, and the wider community is crucial for addressing these challenges and realizing the full potential of blockchain technology.

As we move forward, it is imperative to balance innovation with responsibility, ensuring that blockchain technology serves the broader interests of society. By seizing the opportunities and tackling the challenges, we can shape a future where blockchain technology becomes an integral part of our daily lives, transforming industries, enhancing trust, and driving economic and social progress on a global scale. The journey has just begun, and the possibilities are limitless.

THE END

Key Terms and Definitions

To help you better understand the language and concepts related to aging and older adults, below you will find a list of key terms and their definitions.

Key Terms and Definitions:

1. Cryptocurrency: A digital or virtual form of currency that uses cryptography for secure financial transactions, control the creation of new units, and verify the transfer of assets.

2. Proof-of-Work (PoW): A consensus mechanism used in blockchain networks where participants solve complex mathematical problems to validate transactions and add new blocks to the blockchain.

3. Litecoin (LTC): A peer-to-peer cryptocurrency that was created in 2011 as a "silver to Bitcoin's gold." It shares many similarities with Bitcoin but offers faster transaction confirmation times and a different hashing algorithm.

4. Peercoin (PPC): A cryptocurrency established in 2012 known for its sustainable and energy-efficient design. It introduced the proof-of-stake (PoS) hybrid model, which combines elements of both proof-of-work and proof-of-stake.

5. Bytecoin (BCN): A privacy-focused cryptocurrency established in 2012. It utilizes the Cryptonote protocol and

ring signatures to ensure untraceable and confidential transactions.

6. Monero (XMR): An established cryptocurrency from 2014 that emphasizes privacy, security, and untraceability. It implements technologies such as Ring Confidential Transactions (RingCT) and stealth addresses.

7. Zcash (ZEC): A privacy-protecting digital currency launched in 2016. It utilizes zero-knowledge proofs and zk-SNARKs to enable shielded transactions that offer enhanced privacy and selective transparency.

8. Decentralized Finance (DeFi): An ecosystem of financial applications built on blockchain networks, aiming to provide traditional financial services such as lending, borrowing, and trading in a decentralized manner, without intermediaries.

9. Interoperability: The ability of different blockchain networks and protocols to seamlessly communicate, exchange data, and transfer assets between each other.

10. Sustainability: The consideration of environmental impact and energy efficiency in the design and operation of blockchain networks and cryptocurrencies.

11. Privacy-enhancing Technologies: Tools and techniques implemented in cryptocurrencies and blockchain

networks to protect user privacy and ensure the confidentiality of transactions.

12. Regulatory Frameworks: Laws, regulations, and guidelines established by governments and regulatory bodies to govern the use, trading, and operation of cryptocurrencies and blockchain technology.

13. Education and Awareness: Initiatives aimed at educating individuals, businesses, and policymakers about blockchain technology, its benefits, use cases, and potential risks.

14. Blockchain Analysis: The process of examining and tracking transactions on a blockchain to gain insights, identify patterns, and trace the flow of funds.

15. Future of Blockchain: The potential advancements, challenges, and opportunities that lie ahead for blockchain technology, including its impact on various industries and society as a whole.

Introduction:

Nakamoto, S. (2008). Bitcoin: A Peer-to-Peer Electronic Cash System. Retrieved from https://bitcoin.org/bitcoin.pdf

Chapter 1: Litecoin (LTC), established 2011 - "The silver to Bitcoin's gold."

Lee, C. (2011). Litecoin: Open source P2P digital currency. Retrieved from https://litecoin.org/

Chapter 2: Peercoin (PPC), established 2012 - "Sustainable, energy-efficient cryptocurrency."

King, S., & Nadal, S. (2012). PPCoin: Peer-to-Peer Crypto-Currency with Proof-of-Stake. Retrieved from https://peercoin.net/whitepaper

Chapter 3: Bytecoin (BCN), established 2012 - "Private, untraceable cryptocurrency."

CryptoNote Developers. (2012). CryptoNote v 2.0. Retrieved from https://cryptonote.org/whitepaper.pdf

Chapter 4: Monero (XMR), established 2014 - "Private, secure, and untraceable cryptocurrency."

Monero Research Lab. (2014). Ring Confidential Transactions. Retrieved from https://lab.getmonero.org/pubs/MRL-0005.pdf

Chapter 5: Zcash (ZEC), established 2016 - "Privacy-protecting digital currency."

Sasson, E. B., Chiesa, A., Garman, C., Green, M., Miers, I., Tromer, E., & Virza, M. (2014). Zerocash: Decentralized Anonymous Payments from Bitcoin. Retrieved from https://zerocash-project.org/media/pdf/zerocash-extended-20140518.pdf

Chapter 6: Comparative Analysis and Synergies

Antonopoulos, A. M. (2014). Mastering Bitcoin: Unlocking Digital Cryptocurrencies. O'Reilly Media.

Buterin, V. (2013). Ethereum: A Next-Generation Smart Contract and Decentralized Application Platform. Retrieved from https://github.com/ethereum/wiki/wiki/White-Paper

Chapter 7: The Future of PoW and Beyond

Tapscott, D., & Tapscott, A. (2016). Blockchain Revolution: How the Technology Behind Bitcoin Is Changing Money, Business, and the World. Portfolio.

Antonopoulos, A. M. (2017). Mastering Ethereum: Building Smart Contracts and DApps. O'Reilly Media.

Conclusion:

Popper, N. (2016). Digital Gold: Bitcoin and the Inside Story of the Misfits and Millionaires Trying to Reinvent Money. Harper Paperbacks.

Tapscott, D., & Tapscott, A. (2018). Blockchain Revolution: How the Technology Behind Bitcoin and Other Cryptocurrencies Is Changing the World. Portfolio.